Family Customs and Traditions

Family Customs and Traditions

CYNTHIA MACGREGOR

Fairview Press   *Minneapolis*

Published by Fairview Press, 2450 Riverside Avenue South, Minneapolis, MN 55454.

Library of Congress Cataloging-in-Publication Data

MacGregor, Cynthia, 1943-
    Family customs and traditions / [edited by] Cynthia MacGregor
       p.   cm.
       ISBN 1-57749-004-5 : (pbk : alk. paper)
       1. Family festivals—United States. 2. Holidays—United
    States. 3. United States—Social life and customs. I. MacGregor,
    Cynthia.
GT2402.U6F35 1995
394.2—dc20   95-407
                                          CIP

Printed in the United States of America
99 98 97 96   7 6 5 4 3 2

Cover design and illustration: Circus Design

Publisher's Note: Fairview Press publishes books and other materials related to the subjects of physical health, mental health, and family issues. Its publications, including *Family Customs and Traditions*, do not necessarily reflect the philosophy of Fairview Hospital and Healthcare Services or their treatment programs.

For a free current catalog of Fairview Press titles, please call this toll-free number: 1-800-544-8207.

For the greatest mother in the world, otherwise known as Yvonne Epstein, whose best family tradition was simply lots of love and who always had faith in me— even when I didn't have faith in myself.

And to the memory of my dad, Sam Aronson, who had no shortage of love either.

Contents

Acknowledgments   ix

Introduction   1

Family Harmony   5

Christmas and Chanukah Celebrations   61

Other Traditional Holidays, Birthdays,
and Other Celebrations   99

Invented Holidays   155

Keeping in Touch   169

Traditions Rooted in Superstition   183

Miscellaneous Customs and Traditions   191

Author's Note   213

Acknowledgments

A heartfelt "Thank you" to Vic Bobb, without whose help (not to mention encouragement) this book would have been, at very least, much more difficult and even more time-consuming . . . if it would have happened at all.

Thanks also to all the contributors, those whose names are listed after their contributions as well as those who chose to remain anonymous but without whose input I would not have had a book.

Introduction

What is tradition? Some say it's the glue that holds a family together. A tradition may have its roots in great-great-grandma's time, or it may be something you just decided to start doing last year but plan to continue on a regular basis as time goes on. New traditions are born every day!

And then there are those wonderful little things your family does that you can't quite call traditions, yet they're practices that are important to you and that you're glad to keep up . . . call them family customs. They may be little ways of saying and showing "I love you" or that all-important "I'm proud of you." They may just be special ways your family shares of having fun.

Fun is important, too. It provides every family member with a sense of well-being, promotes a sense of family togetherness, and gives ample fodder for fond recollection years later: "Remember the time when _____?" "Remember how we always used to _____?"

Many customs and traditions among families concern ways of celebrating holidays, birthdays, and other special occasions. Other traditions make any day a special occasion. Still others, equally important, are simply that particular family's unique way of dealing with all the old bugaboos—chores, bedtime, and other words that bring a frown to the faces of most kids. If handled with grace and a deft touch, even bedtimes and chore times can result in memories a child will treasure and seek to replicate with his or her children in later years.

And, after all, you're really doing more than constructing memories; you're cementing relationships. Today, "dysfunctional" is a household word, and the number of divorced people in the U.S. numbers close to 16,000,000. In these days, when both fragmented families and as-yet-together families that are still coming apart at the seams are all too common, we need all the help we can get.

A well-known religious advertisement has it that "The family that prays together stays together," but truly it takes more than prayer to keep a family intact—and intact in more than legality. And what of families that aren't religious—surely there is cement to hold those families together as well!

I offer no simplistic panacea. Surely, the institution of a tradition isn't going to make all the difference between a happy childhood and a miserable one, between a successful marriage and a failure . . . but, hey, it's a start! Family traditions promote togetherness, foster happy memories, and engender warm feelings in the hearts of all involved. Can you beat that?! Too, many of the traditions and customs in this book specifically deal with family togetherness, or with means by which far-flung or extended families can keep in touch.

What if you're already divorced? Take heart—a "family" can be one parent and one or more kids, too. Quite a few of the people who contributed to this book are divorced—as am I— but unquestionably they and their kids can still be a family— and if the family is fragmented, that's all the more reason the family needs a solid foundation upon which to be grounded. Traditions can form a substantial part of that foundation.

If you're a divorced parent, consider this: Your child's strongest memories of childhood, in years to come, don't have to be of the night you or your ex-spouse left; they can just as easily be of the year you started the new tradition, of the special ornaments that graced your every Christmas tree, of the blueberry pie you baked every Thanksgiving, defying universal tradition, because your tradition was to bake your child's favorite.

Or of the "jigsaw letters," cut apart in puzzle fashion, that you sent your child at camp, which had to be assembled before they could be read—your family's own custom—or of the weekly visits to the library, followed by ice cream (to instill in the kids the association that reading is sweet), or whatever your own family's traditions and customs are . . . or will be after reading this book.

Many of the traditions in this book gently teach a lesson, too. In a world where, often, we're shocked by violence, enraged at rage, and astounded at lack of human decency, kids need all the grounding in compassion and human kindness they can get. And they'll find some of it among some of the traditions in this book.

The customs and traditions in this book aren't the old familiar ethnic or religious ones; they're individual families' own traditions and customs, garnered from people all across America. These people spoke about traditions started out of love, out of a sense of family, out of pride, out of necessity, out of desire to instill good values in their children, a few that started out of superstition. One even started as a practical joke.

To amass this information, I placed ads in various publications, sent out a form letter to virtually everyone in my address book and Rolodex (a formidable list!), and advertised extensively on-line, traveling the Information Superhighway to "meet" people all across the U.S., with a few contributions from people in Canada and overseas as well. I never knew, when I logged on every morning, where the ad responses would pop up from. Hong Kong? Scotland? Austria? Australia?

You won't read in this book about kissing under the mistletoe, or about the groom and his mother or the bride and her father dancing together. Those are everybody's traditions. This book is about particular families' traditions, traditions that only the Joneses, the O'Reillys, the Blooms, or the Sorensens take part in, traditions not fostered or officially sanctioned by any ethnic or religious group—in fact by any organized group at all, except the Joneses, the O'Reillys, the Blooms, or the Sorensens, whatever family contributed that particular custom to this book. But these are traditions that, now that you've read about them, your family may want to borrow from the families that contributed them.

It's certainly my hope that within this book you'll find several or many traditions you'd like to institute in your family. You may be inspired by an item in here to think of something similar but different you want to try, a whole new tradition that will be unique to your family. Some of the items shared in this book may bring a smile to your face, or a warm glow—perhaps the glow of remembrance—to your heart. Traditions, after all, are family ties.

But whether this book evokes memories of your childhood or inspires you to start new customs or traditions for your own family, I hope you enjoy reading it as much as I've enjoyed compiling it. And to all the people who shared their families' customs and traditions with me, whether I was able to use their offerings in the book or not, a heartfelt "Thank you!"

Family Harmony

So many of the traditions that hold a family together and make it special are centered not around a big occasion or a special holiday but around everyday happenings. Quick—what's your favorite memory of your own childhood? It might be of a tall, fragrant, fresh-cut Christmas tree or your mom's home-baked birthday cakes, but the chances are awfully good it's of some far more ordinary, prosaic, everyday happening.

The ways we deal with commonplace events may seem trivial at the time, but often our so-called "ordinary" behavior weaves the fabric of cherished memories that will warm our children's hearts in years to come. Whether it's afternoons moms and daughters spend making jelly together, evenings with the whole family gathered around the fireplace telling family history, or a special bedtime ritual that neatly gives closure to a day of mixed emotions and eases the way to sleep, these so-called "little things" can seem awfully big in retrospect as they burn brightly among our storehouse of reminiscences. And these special moments, treasured in reminiscence by parents and children alike in years to come, are more important to our children right now than we often suspect at the time.

Family History at Bedtime

Of course my kids like to hear bedtime stories before I tuck them in every night. We cuddle in the living room and I tell them a favorite story or read them a book, or part of one. But Sunday night bedtime stories are special. I set Sundays aside for telling them family history.

It might be a story from when I was a little girl, or a recounting of my wedding to their father, although more often it goes back even further than that, but it's always family history. They've heard something about everyone in the family photo albums, so the faces in the pictures all have meaning for them. They know about Great-Grandma's journey to America on the boat, about how Grandpa started a business with no money, the funny story of Aunt Ellen and the mule, and the family version of the Biblical "begats"—who is the child of whom, and the grandchild of whom, and so on.

Some of the stories are old favorites that they request over and over. Some, less interesting to them, are nevertheless important for them to hear, though they don't get repeated as frequently. Naturally they're more interested in hearing about relatives they know, names they can relate to. But I make sure they hear facts about everyone in the family that I know something about.

My children are growing up with a sense of family and a family pride. And they look forward to our Sunday just-before-bedtime ritual.

Anonymous

"The G____ Family Follies"

⋙+⋘

When my brother was around eight, he saw Sammy Davis, Jr. on TV—I think it may have been on the "Ed Sullivan Show"—and got it into his head that he wanted to be a tap-dancer too. After much coaxing, he persuaded Mom and Dad to sign him up for tap lessons. There was only one other boy in his class, but he persevered for three years until adolescence, and the withdrawal of that only other boy in the class embarrassed him into dropping out.

So he never became a white Sammy Davis, Jr., or an Italian Gene Kelly, or whatever. In fact, today he's an architect, which is pretty far removed from the performing arts. But his tap lessons led to the inception of the "G____ Family Follies."

It started when he was rehearsing for his end-of-year recital at the dance school. He loved dancing but was nervous at the thought of getting up and dancing in front of his first audience.

"Why don't you practice by dancing for us," Dad suggested. "Put on a show."

That's when my other brother, then around five, chimed in, "I wanna be in the show too."

Dad's response was, "This is your brother's show," but my mom had a different take on it.

She said, "Let everybody participate. Let's make it a whole-family thing." I was taking violin lessons at the time, and my mom saw this as a chance to encourage me to perform (the music school where I studied didn't give recitals) and perhaps to get me to practice more, too.

So we all participated—Mom and Dad too. Dad was a self-taught pianist. He had a natural ear and could pick out any pop song easily without the sheet music—and I don't mean just playing with one finger, either. Mom had learned guitar as a teenager. My tap-dancing brother did his thing, and the younger brother got out his junior magician kit and regaled the rest of us with a few ineptly performed tricks. I played my violin.

It was good for us, and it was fun. The following week, the younger of my brothers wanted to do it again, so we did. After that it became a regular once-a-month occurrence. The first Sunday of the month, at 7 PM, we presented "The G_____ Family Follies," with each of us performing in whatever way we could. The "magician" sometimes sang instead of performing tricks, and eventually he persuaded my parents to enroll him, too, in music school, where he studied drums. This made for some very noisy Sunday evenings!

But the shows developed our poise and self-confidence and encouraged us to practice, practice, practice. Our parents, though adoring, were also critical. They could be proud of us and still point out places where our performances were rough around the edges. As the oldest, I came in for the most criticism; they naturally expected more of me.

Though the performances were usually put on by the five of us for only the five of us, occasional visiting grandparents or other relatives got to see some of our shows, and slowly we began inviting friends to view us from time to time as well. We kids were quite the hams, and in retrospect I'd have to say that Mom and Dad enjoyed showing off too!

My brother the former magician swears that those early performances in "The G_____ Family Follies" prepared him for the public speaking he now does in connection with his work. None of us three kids went into show business, but we all enjoyed putting on shows. I believe those shows were beneficial to each of us, in one way or another, beyond just getting us to practice violin/tap dance/drums/whatever more than we otherwise might have.

Family Customs and Traditions

I'm in my late twenties, and still single, but if I ever do have a family, I intend to push my kids gently in the direction of learning some performance craft and putting on family shows on Sunday evenings. I'd better brush up on my violin skills, just in case.

Anonymous

Learning at Work with Dad

My husband, Dan, is very good about spending time with our children every night after supper, whether playing games, wrestling, reading, or whatever; we also go to church with them when they go to Sunday school, instead of just dropping them off at the door.

But Dan also spends time with the kids during working hours whenever he gets a chance. He works for a lumber company, designing horse barns and riding arenas around New England, and sometimes he has the opportunity to take one of the kids with him on a trip in the truck during working hours.

Because the kids are learning at home, and not in nursery school, this doesn't disrupt their schooling or anybody's carpool arrangements.

It's interesting for the kids, because the places they go to tend to be farms, horse farms, and places under construction, all of which they find interesting. Once every two months or so, one of the kids gets to go with him.

The kids get to see what Dad does for a living and how a house or barn is built; they also get to see a lot of animals. Dan usually takes them out for lunch that day as well.

We hope to develop this custom into Date Night with Mom or Dad later. I know a woman with seven children under 8 (his, hers, and theirs) who has a date with each child once in the summer. They get to choose bowling, Chuck E. Cheese, or some other treat.

Sherry Yeaton
Epsom, New Hampshire

A Scrapbook of Memories for Each

In our family, we encouraged the children from an early age to each keep a scrapbook of his or her own, filled with mementos of special outings, family trips, school awards, Sunday school awards, even pressed flowers picked while on an extended-family picnic. This was something my mother had us do when my brother and I were little, and I've carried the tradition on with my kids.

The kids enjoy looking at my old scrapbook, too. It reminds them that I was a child once, an important realization for kids to have about their parents, and it lets them see me as a person, not just as a mommy. I only wish my husband had a scrapbook of his own to share with the kids.

I started the kids' scrapbooks for them the day they were born. The announcement of each of their births is the first item in each one. (Another copy of each birth announcement resides in my scrapbook as well. Yes, I still keep my scrapbook up through my adult years.)

The scrapbook I started in my childhood is filled mostly with reminders of happy events, but there's an important sad event or two commemorated there as well: my father's and grandmother's death announcements are in there, and the tags of several childhood pets who died. The same will be true of my children's scrapbooks too, I'm sure, but even so I believe that when that time comes, they'll be learning the important lesson that death and loss are an inevitable part of life.

Meanwhile, I'm happy to report that the only rather sad items in my kids' scrapbooks so far are things like the second-place prize certificate from the spelling bee my daughter won when she really wanted to win first prize but missed a word, and other reminders of similar childhood disappointments.

My son has elected to mix photos in with his other mementos, rather than keep them in a separate photo album; he calls the shots because it's his scrapbook. It's important for the kids to understand that the scrapbooks are theirs to keep, theirs to keep up, and theirs to decide on the contents.

If something they want to preserve strikes me as inconsequential, it's not for me to prevent them from including it. I may voice an opinion from time to time, but they're the final arbiters of what goes into the scrapbooks. This reinforces the feeling that the scrapbooks are truly theirs, and that the scrapbooks reflect their lives. This keeps the kids' interest in the scrapbooks high, and I'm sure they'll still be adding to them, and poring over them, on into their adult years—just as I still do with mine.

Anonymous

1-4-3

When my stepdad was courting my mom, they talked by phone during the workday and wanted to say "I love you" to each other at the close of their conversations. For my mom, this was no problem; she had a reasonable amount of privacy in the office where she worked. But my stepdad owned a store, and all the guys who worked for him could overhear his conversations. He didn't even let them know he was talking to a woman—he certainly couldn't say "I love you."

So instead he said, "1-4-3." There is one letter in the word "I," and four and three respectively in "love" and "you." So "1-4-3" was code for "I love you." It caught on in the family, and soon "1-4-3" became familyspeak for "I love you" even when no code was needed.

To this day, my mom, my stepdad, my daughter, and I all use it intermittently. A letter from my daughter is as apt to close with "1-4-3" as with "Love," and my mom, signing off on the phone, may well end the conversation with "1-4-3" in lieu of "I love you."

C.M.

"Good-Night" / "Good-bye"

Saying "good-bye" was and still remains important in our family.

Because "good-bye" will, at one point in time, like it or not, hold the position of being a last good-bye, it has always been treated with a bit of sanctity and reverence. Even at age thirty-eight, I still kiss my grandmother on the cheek before I leave her home and kiss my mother on the cheek as well. In fact, I'm so accustomed to this ritual that it's hard to conceive that some other people don't do this.

As for my mother, when you leave her home and are pulling out of the driveway, she always stands at the door waving a buoyant good-bye with her long, willowy arms. Sometimes I used to wonder whether she was just glad to see people leave.

But the art of saying good-bye came full circle in our family about eight years ago, when I stood in the funeral home after my father had died of cancer. It was the first night of his being laid out. It was nearing time for the funeral home to close for the night, and all the rest of the friends and family had graciously left, leaving my mother, my sister, and me in the funeral home for a few quiet moments alone.

Without thinking, my sister and I walked toward the coffin. At about the same time, we realized we were heading up to give our dad a good-night kiss. We looked at one another sadly, our eyes exchanging the knowledge that perhaps all those moments as children, when our friends thought it was silly to kiss our parents good-bye and good-night, had really not been so silly after all.

Leaning over, I gave my father a kiss for good-night. Then I went home.

Teresa Alexander
Hazel Park, Michigan

Family Customs and Traditions

Family Prayer

My family believed in saying grace before meals, and each night it was a different person's turn to say it, but we never said a "standard" grace, a formal prayer that anyone had learned at church or at a friend's house. It had to be original and from the heart.

Now, of course there was a limit to how original these prayers could be night after night. They often ran to "Thank you for this food and a loving family" or words to that effect. But at least they were what we felt at the time. And if what we felt was "Thank you that I didn't fail that history test," well then that was what we said.

It's funny, because we weren't an especially church-going family. We attended for Christmas and a few other times a year when my folks got the notion that "this would be a nice weekend to go to church." (I never knew, and still don't, what prompted those decisions.) But my parents definitely believed in God, and we were brought up to believe that God was always listening and should be thanked for all blessings.

In my mind, I equated grace at dinner with the thank-you notes we had to send after getting birthday and Christmas presents. If someone gave you a present, it was proper to sit down and let them know you appreciated it. If God gave you a pretty day, a snowfall that was good for sledding, a good family to live in, or an especially yummy-smelling dinner (in which case you can believe we kept the grace real short!), it was proper to give thanks for it, too.

We also learned to thank God for the things we didn't want and didn't get—like the year the chicken pox was going around, and almost all our friends got it, but no one in our family did.

Anonymous

The Bible as a Way of Life

✥

We began a tradition ten years ago, when my son was six months old. We wanted all our children to know about the Bible, so we began reading it on a daily basis. Although we are Christian, we adopted the Jewish tradition of making the Bible a way of life.

Every day after breakfast we use a devotional magazine called *Open Windows*. Usually my wife reads a portion of Scripture and the comments that follow in the guide. Our children listen. After we read, we discuss it and try to apply it to our everyday living.

As our children have grown, they have sometimes asked to read the Scripture. They now view it as an important part of life. They also did not realize for a long time that not everyone reads the Bible. They thought that everyone reads it every day.

Mike McGuire
Laredo, Texas

Dad on His Knees

My father passed away in January of '94 from Parkinson's Disease. I spent his last days with him at the hospital. It's funny how, sitting there, you reflect on your whole life and remember things you hadn't thought about for many years.

Above all, I remember how every night my dad would kneel by his bed and say his prayers. That always touched me, and I too knelt by my bed at night to give thanks for the day.

What a wonderful example he set for me! He continued to kneel by his bed every night until he became bed-bound, but I know that even after that, every night as he lay in his bed, he thanked the good Lord for another day.

Bill Malcom
Roanoke, Virginia

A Good Send-off

My family were coal miners and part-time farmers. Whenever the miners in the family left for work, the whole rest of the family would line up to wish them goodbye. We'd all say "Be careful ___," adding the miner's name and pronouncing "careful" as "keerful."

Miners were often injured or killed in the mines, and we wanted to make sure our family got a good send-off for what might be the last time they were seen alive.

Herbert D. Tabor
South Houston, Texas

Family Book Night

My parents were both great readers; when they had even a few spare minutes, if they weren't working a crossword, they read. To instill the same love of literature in us, they declared Sunday nights Family Book Nights.

Each child was expected to read one book a week—books assigned in school didn't count—and to report on it in some way on Sunday night. The report could be either written and read aloud; oral and informal; or something more creative. The more creative reports included puppet shows, drawings of key scenes in the book with accompanying verbal explanations, and dramatic readings of selected passages.

It wasn't uncommon for our father to quiz us on the books we'd read, to verify that we'd really read the whole book, and not just the beginning, the end, and a chapter in the middle.

When we were little, just learning to read, a picture book was certainly acceptable as our weekly book; as we got older, we were expected to read longer and more difficult books.

You might think that we'd grow to hate reading as a result of having it forced on us like so much extra homework (and I don't deny a fair amount of grumbling when the need to read conflicted head-on with a stickball game in progress, or a chance to shoot hoops at the gym). However, we grew up with exactly the love of reading my dad had hoped to foster in us, as well as an appreciation of our parents for teaching us to enjoy books.

Anonymous

Family Nights

Because we were disappointed with the programming on television, we started our own video library. We purchased several Disney tapes and other cartoons like the Jetsons, Yogi Bear, and Bugs Bunny.

On Friday night we have family night. One child selects what we will do. It may be to watch one of the cartoon videos, or to play a card game or board game, or to go to the park if weather permits. Sometimes we go to the fast food restaurants that have playground equipment. We get dessert and let the kids play.

On Saturdays, we watch "Dr. Quinn, Medicine Woman" on TV. That has become our youngest daughter's favorite program. This is also a family time.

Mike McGuire
Laredo, Texas

Uncle Wiggily and Ice Cream

When I was a kid, my parents used to like to take my brother and me for car rides in the country. My parents often read a storybook to us about Uncle Wiggily, a rabbit who went adventuring, so on our car rides we'd go to the country and go adventuring like Uncle Wiggily.

Often my father would pretend he was lost, though it was all a game and he really wasn't lost at all. We'd wind up in the most remarkable places, including interesting restaurants way out in the country. Or, often, my mother would have a picnic dinner hidden in the back of the car, and we'd eat dinner outdoors in the countryside.

Or we'd accidentally-on-purpose wind up at wonderful ice-cream places.

Linda Becker
West Palm Beach, Florida

Library Outings

One custom in our family is going to the library weekly. When I was a kid, my dad took us religiously every Saturday. Our limit was ten books, and I love to read. Now I take my boys. We go at least once a week, sometimes two or three times a week. I think it's the most important thing I have done for them educationally.

I let them take out as many books as they like, and I read to them. Even when Joel was tiny, I would bring him to the library with me, show him all the neat decorations, and tell him what a fun place it was.

Our boys both love to be read to and to look at books. The librarians sometimes look strangely at our pile of twenty-four books, but our library has no limit, and one librarian told me, "Actually it boosts our circulation—keep it up!"

Sherry Yeaton
Epsom, New Hampshire

Help for Good Habits from the Tooth Fairy

We wanted our children to learn to care for their teeth properly, so when our son's first tooth fell out, we left a new toothbrush with the dollar "from the tooth fairy." When his second tooth fell out, the toothbrush was still in good shape, but we felt we'd started something meaningful by leaving that toothbrush with the first dollar, and we wanted to carry on the custom.

So we left some sugarless gum and a couple of bags of healthy snacks under the pillow with the dollar. We were getting further away from good *dental* health now, the snacks being more nutrition-oriented, but good overall health is important, too.

Our daughter's first tooth was next to fall out, and she got a new toothbrush, the same as our son had with his first tooth that fell out.

Our dentist has some booklets for kids with information about proper dental care, along with pictures to color in to make it interesting for kids, and that's what our son and daughter each got with their tooth fairy money for their next teeth that fell out.

Our daughter got bubble bath with her next dollar. She's a bit of a tomboy and down on baths. We thought the bubble bath would encourage her to bathe happily and stay in the tub longer, and we were right, so we chalked that up to good hygiene and felt we'd done the right thing again.

Most of our successive "tooth fairy" gifts to our children have ranged even further afield from dental health, though a new toothbrush does pop up with the dollar whenever the timing's right. We have broadened our scope to include good overall health, good grooming, and even good habits. The tooth fairy has left gifts unheard of in most households, but our kids (now seven and eight) still believe in her and enjoy the gifts she leaves them, which always include (besides the dollar for the tooth), something to promote either dental hygiene, good overall health, neat habits, or some other positive trait.

Anonymous

Pomegranate Jellymaking and More

My grandfather came to California when he was very young, and he grew pomegranates in his yard. One of my earliest memories is of being out in the back yard, watching the family (all four of his kids, their spouses, their kids, and a few neighbors) picking pomegranates off the trees, cutting them, squeezing them, making jelly, jarring it, and sealing the jars. It was time for the whole family to come together and to talk about everything as they worked.

My father often told me of stories he'd heard from Grandpa about when he was a boy in the early 1900s. I often wished Grandpa would tell me some stories, but I was mostly content to listen to him sing old cowboy songs. He and all of his children played guitar very well; it was like being in church.

I still don't think I've ever heard a sound as beautiful as my father singing with Grandpa, Aunt Shirley (Noel), and Uncles Bill and Gerry Bollman. The songs told stories of lost loves on the lonesome prairie and could make you cry. (It's no easy feat to get an eleven-year-old in a melancholy mood.) Grandpa died in 1978, and we miss him greatly. He was the glue that held my family together, and I think that today his memory still acts as the glue for us.

Rik Bollman
Nevada

Toys in "Toy Jail" as Punishment

When my son, Rhys, (fifteen months old) is naughty and gets a "time-out," his punishment is that one of his toys has to go to "toy jail." He waves bye to it, and away it goes. We have two "toy jails"; one is a big cardboard box, but we also use the closet, because he's too young to reach the doorknob yet. Sometimes there are quite a few toys in "jail."

When Rhys is good and has a day with no time-outs, he gets one toy back. He doesn't like to see the toys disappear into the closet or box, and he's very happy when they come out.

Right now he has no conception of what "jail" is—to him it's that box or the closet. But when he's older, we're going to make a box that truly looks like a jail, complete with cut-out bars.

Jomil Mulvey
San Diego, California

Family Customs and Traditions

Food for the Mind

I grew up in a family of seven children. Our parents were very big on education, and at the table after supper we'd talk about what we'd learned that day, starting with the oldest child. Dad would ask a question on a topic we'd learned that day, and if we didn't know the answer, we'd have to get him an answer by the next night. Only if we knew the answer would we be excused from the table to go out and play.

On weekends, when there was no school, the kids younger than us would ask us a question on either math or spelling, and we'd have to answer it before we could be excused from the table. Some nights we ended up sitting at that table for a long time!

As far as report cards went, my brothers and sisters and I would always look at each other's report cards and try to offer ways to help each other in the areas in which we were weak, so education really became a family affair; we were all very concerned with each other's success in school. As a consequence, all seven children went to the University and got good educations.

To this day, I carry the habit forward. I try to talk to my wife at the dinner table about what we've learned that day, although now that I'm older it's more about people than about other facts. I probably learn more at my dinner table than I do during the rest of the day!

Owen Schwer
Edmonton, Alberta, Canada

Family Pillow Fights

Though my parents were born on this side of the ocean, they were strict in a way I eventually characterized (mentally) as "old-world strictness." Still, despite their unequivocal demand for respect and obedience, they were able to have fun and let their hair down when the occasion was appropriate.

One way in which they did this was family pillow fights. From time to time one of them would grab a pillow—perhaps while tucking one of us in bed, perhaps while stripping the bed to do the laundry, perhaps while doing something else in one of the bedrooms—and the fight would be on.

Wham! Whap! Out of nowhere, a pillow would come flying, catching one of us unaware. "Gotcha!" my mom or dad would yell, and of course the target would retaliate, sending a well-aimed pillow back at the parental instigator.

Maybe it was specifically because of the intense demand for respect and the consistent strictness that they imposed on us that the pillow fights were such fun. It was a time when we could get back at Mom and Dad, get even with them, and treat them in a rough-and-tumble way . . . all in good fun, of course. Naturally, my brother and I threw plenty of pillows at each other, as well. Mom and Dad weren't the only targets, not by a long shot. But they were the primary ones.

I doubt they'd read any books on child psychology, but I suspect they understood on a gut level that we were letting out a lot of tensions and aggressions through play.

No matter whose room the fight erupted in, it spread to include everyone. Perhaps Mom would throw the first pillow at my brother, but the mayhem that resulted soon drew Dad and me running to join in the fray. My brother was good at ducking flying pillows, and his raucous catcalls when parents missed their aim left no doubt that a pillow fight was in progress. I'd even put down a good Nancy Drew mystery in the middle of a page to jump in.

I had friends whose parents weren't nearly as strict as ours were. I frankly envied them. But none of their parents let their hair down enough to get into a pillow fight with them, and I was unabashedly proud of my folks for their ability to be child-like enough to instigate the bedlam.

When I had my two sons, I made sure to get into pillow fights with them (they loved it!), and now that I have a six-month-old granddaughter, I'm merely in a holding pattern. She'll be old enough soon enough.

I'm not too old for pillow fights, and I'll never make the mistake of thinking I'm too dignified. Nobody should be. My strict but fun-loving parents understood that.

Anonymous

Sunday Night Dinner/Discussions

Growing up in the '60s and '70s as I did, our dinner was some-times catch-as-catch-can. We didn't always eat together—my Girl Scout meetings or band practice, my brother's football practice or club involvements, my father's need to see business clients some evenings, and my mother's need to drive us all over the place all intervened. Many nights we weren't together for dinner as a full family, and some nights none of us ate together.

Except Sundays. My father had an ironclad rule about Sundays. No business, no activities, no anything could interfere with the one night the family had dinner all together. We couldn't make dates with friends for Sunday nights either. Sunday night was family night.

Dinner was promptly at 6:00. During dinner, we talked between bites (but never with our mouths full!), and after din-ner the dishes were cleared (by all of us) and left to soak in the sink. Then we really talked. If there was something important in the way of family business, this was often the time it was brought up. Had my parents planned a vacation for us? Was my mom going to work part-time? Were my brother's grades unac-ceptable? Were we going to get a new car? Chances are, Sunday nights were when we heard about it.

If one of us had a question, problem, or gripe, Sunday night was the best time to bring it up. Not that my parents wouldn't listen at any other time, and certainly problems of an urgent nature were dealt with as they came up. But we were encour-aged to bring to the table, after Sunday dinner, any topic that merited discussion, ranging from family problems to our views of world situations.

Family Customs and Traditions

If we had no pressing family business, that didn't mean we could run off and play. In that case, my father proposed a topic of conversation and off we went. It might be world hunger or some other current event, or it might be a lively discussion of ethics. My father would throw hypothetical situations at us: Is it right to _____? Then he'd throw a monkey wrench in the works: Well, what if _____? If my brother and I didn't answer voluntarily, he'd call on us, sometimes making us think we were back in the classroom.

If I'd brought an ethics problem to Mom during the week, she might raise the question for discussion after Sunday night dinner. One example was the time I saw a friend cheat on an exam, then didn't speak up when the teacher asked us to report any cheating we had witnessed. I felt torn. On the one hand, the teacher had asked us to report cheating and I hadn't. On the other hand, the miscreant in question was a friend, and I didn't want to rat on her. Friends don't rat on friends. Had I done wrong? Or would I have been more wrong had I reported on the cheating friend?

Mom threw that situation open for family discussion one Sunday night. All sides of the question were thrown open for appraisal and evaluation. It was at Sunday evening table that I first learned that the world and its problems aren't black and white; there are a lot of shades of gray, too. A clear-cut right and wrong do not exist in every situation.

Our manners at Sunday dinner had to be impeccable, too. A certain degree of sloppy manners was overlooked the other six nights—assuming no company was present—but no elbows were allowed on the table on Sunday, nor could we reach for something that was at all nearer to someone else. If the salt, the gravy, the peas, or whatever were nearer someone else, we had to say, "Please pass the ___," even if we could reach it without getting out of our chairs.

"Our kids are going to be able to go out in the world without embarrassing us . . . and without having to be embarrassed themselves over not knowing proper manners," my parents said assertively. On Sunday nights we used both dinner forks and salad forks, and we were expected to use the right ones at the right times, even if on other nights we used the same fork for both. Utensils were to be used impeccably correctly, and there was no sopping up gravy with bread.

We were not excused from the table till Dad said so— except temporarily, to use the bathroom if needed, of course. Sometimes we grumbled, especially if it was the first warm evening of spring and we wanted to be out with our friends, freed from the drudgery of winter indoors. Or if a party was on at a friend's house, or when a really good TV show was on, or something else that was awfully tempting. But considering that we were excused from having dinner with the family for any even semi-good reason the other six nights of the week, we knew we had little to gripe about.

And as we spent more and more time out in the world as we got older, we appreciated the training we'd gotten from our parents those Sunday evenings. We'd not only gotten a good grounding in table etiquette but also learned how to converse at the dinner table and how to have somewhat sensible views on current events, world affairs, and other things that were discussed in the "real world."

In short, we were prepared for the world. And I'm grateful.

Anonymous

Tucking Mommy In

Part of the time when my children were growing up—the oldest was about twelve, and the others younger—I was divorced. I used to go to bed earlier than they did, and they got into the habit of tucking me into bed every night, instead of my tucking them in. This was very special to me.

Gracie Newsom
Benton, Tennessee

An Old-Fashioned Family

My family has a devotional time after supper nearly every evening. When everyone is finished eating, I read a chapter from the Bible. Sometimes the kids have questions about what is read or something that is suggested by the reading. We try to encourage discussion about ideas and discourage destructive criticism about people.

My wife still puts all the kids to bed at night—even our oldest, a sixteen-year-old boy. It is a cherished tradition with my wife, and sometimes I get into the act too, but I tend to stir the kids up and get them excited rather than settling them into bed.

My wife talks to them, sometimes at length, about their day and any problems. She gives advice and generally comforts them. She may take thirty minutes, just sitting there talking or simply being quiet and lending the comfort of her presence while the boys drift off to sleep. All of our boys say a prayer at night, and their prayers are very enlightening about what is on their minds.

Our daughter was killed five years ago. We have an 8.5" x 11" photo that has a permanent place on the mantle of the fireplace. We have kept her room exactly as it was before she was killed. We go to our daughter's grave on holidays and put flowers on her grave. It is a family affair. Though it's not a happy time, it's something that we must do.

Our family goes to church three times a week, and we require our boys to be home in time to get ready to go. If they stay overnight Saturday with a friend, they must be home by 8:30 on Sunday morning. Sunday afternoon they must be home by 5 PM so they can get ready for church again.

Family Customs and Traditions

My mother lives in Alabama. We live in Ohio. On Christmas, Memorial Day, Thanksgiving, and Labor Day, we usually go to Grandma's house in Alabama. Sometimes my siblings and their families visit her on these holidays too. Whoever gets there first gets to sleep in the Blue Room. Late arrivals may have to sleep on the floor, or on the couch in the kitchen, where you are the last to be able to get to sleep and the first awakened in the morning. On Sunday everyone gets up and goes to church. We take up a whole pew or more in church. The congregation is always glad to see us.

James Johnson
Dayton, Ohio

Amusing Sister

When my half-sister was born, I was nine years old and in the third grade. For a while I was jealous because I had always been the youngest, but the jealousy didn't last.

We all took turns feeding her, changing her diapers, and putting her to bed. When I told her bedtime stories, sometimes I would act out nursery rhymes for her with my step-sister, who was only one year older than I. We would dress up in makeshift costumes and make believe we really were in those nursery rhymes.

My half-sister was my best friend when I was growing up, and even though I rarely talk to her now, she will always hold a special place in my heart. We shared a room. We shared our lives.

Anonymous

Reminiscence Night

Our kids' favorite stories are stories about themselves when they were younger, and every once in a while they'll ask us when it's going to be Reminiscence Night again. Pretty soon after that, my wife and I find a night when the kids don't have school the next day and don't have any sleepovers planned, when we don't have plans either. Then we declare Reminiscence Night, and we drag out the family photo albums and videotapes.

Because my wife and I are both prolific though amateur photographers, we have an abundance of albums filled with pictures of the kids and ourselves on any occasion that seemed remotely an excuse for pictures: birthdays, holidays, family excursions, first day of school, snowfalls, you name it.

On Reminiscence Nights, we and the kids gather around in a circle on the living room floor, spread out the albums, and start a chorus of remember-whens. Many pictures spark memories, and anyone is entitled to jump in with, "Remember my third-grade class play? I was the chimney," or "Here's my sixth-grade picnic. You guys were the chaperones," or "Was that my tenth birthday or eleventh? The one where the clown came to the party?" In any case, the initial sentence is usually followed by a string of associated memories.

Often one child's memory sparks another child's memory of his or her birthday, class play, or other occasion. Sometimes we don't spend much time looking at pictures; verbal reminiscences take up most of the evenings. Other times, the kids are more into the pictures and keep the stories to a minimum. The home videos don't seem to provoke quite the same level of conversation, but they do elicit more exclamations of the "Oh, look!" variety.

Invariably the kids stay up past their bedtimes, but there's no school the next day, and we can afford to be a bit permissive.

Occasionally the kids ask to see photos from our childhoods. Mostly they'd rather see their own childhoods than ours, but once in a while they ask for our old photos or our wedding pictures. We're glad to share our childhood stories with them and to give them a sense of their parents as people, not just parents. People who had birthdays, first days of school, joys and sorrows, expectations and disappointments, best friends, boyfriends, and girlfriends, just as our kids do.

Anonymous

Chore Tree

＝≺┼ ╁≻＝

We've taught our children (three boys) that they have to earn what they get in the way of money; they learned that lesson at an early age.

Rather than impose an ever-greater array of chores on our children as they grew older, with allowance linked to performance of those chores, we've come up with a different system. Each of our boys has a very basic list of chores he's expected to do: Make his bed, clean his room, help clear the table. For this he gets a bare-bones allowance. If he wants more money, he has to earn it. Just like in the real world!

We have two bulletin boards in the kitchen. One is for general messages and notes. The other is our "chore tree." My husband cut a sort of tree shape out of construction paper. We already had a whole lot of leaf-shaped pieces of paper left over from a promotion he had at his store a couple of years ago. But one could just as well use plain pieces of paper directly on a bulletin board. You don't really need a "tree" and "leaves."

Whenever my husband or I have a chore around the house or yard that we want to delegate to one of the kids, we write down the chore and what it's worth in points on a piece of "leaf" paper, and tack it up on the chore tree. A child who wants to do that chore and earn those points takes the leaf from the "chore tree" and performs the required task. When it's complete, he gets one of us to inspect the job he did, then sign off on the leaf.

Sunday night is pay night, when the kids present us with their chore leaves for the week. We tally up the points they've earned. For every twenty points they get a dollar. A chore can be worth as little as five points (for a very easy, very brief chore), or as much as two hundred points in extraordinary circumstances.

When buying a new comic book or game cartridge is dependent on earning money, and earning is linked to doing chores, you'd be surprised how willing to work a trio of boys can be: doing inside chores like ironing and silver-polishing, as well as outside chores like leaf-raking or bush-pruning.

I am confident that we are raising boys who know the value of a dollar, who know that you don't get something for nothing in this world, and who are growing up learning household skills, too.

Anonymous

Chore Lottery

For several years my three children squabbled over the after-dinner chores of washing and putting away the dishes. When the two oldest were younger, and the youngest was too young to be expected to help, the two alternated nights. One night, one child washed the dishes while the other, after the dishes had drained dry, put them away. The next night, they traded places. When the youngest got a little older, he was included in the rotation, with one child getting a "free" night.

But there was so much squabbling! "No fair! He got a 'free' night when there was a zillion dishes and I had to wash. Now I've got a 'free' night and he only has to do a few dishes and I got cheated. No fair!" Not to mention the usual, "It's your turn to wash. I washed last night." "Did not! You washed two nights ago."

We solved it all with the lottery, an idea my aunt used successfully for years with her kids. We have three pieces of paper identical in size. On one is written WASH, on one PUT AWAY, and on the third FREE. All three are folded identically, then dropped in a bowl. Each night, each child draws one piece of paper and does whatever chore he has drawn.

True, one child might be stuck with washing the dishes for three nights in a row, or another might be chore-free after dinner for several nights running. But you know what? Life's like that, and the kids are learning that life isn't always fair . . . but that, if you get bad luck this week, or this month, who's to say good luck isn't lurking right around the corner?! Despite the grumbling we hear over "He got FREE the last two nights already!" there's a lot less fussing and complaining than there was under the old system.

Family Customs and Traditions

I think my aunt had the right idea, and now that the kids are old enough to handle the laundry chores, we're going to have another set of lottery slips: WASH, FOLD, and PUT AWAY. (I'm still sticking myself with the job of ironing . . . at least for this year.)

Anonymous

Family Customs and Traditions

Movie Lottery

＝≍‖≍＝

With four kids, we've had quite a few fights over which movie to see on any given weekend. This one wants to see one move, that one wants to see another, the third says, "But we've seen that twice! Let's see this one instead!" And the fourth, who wanted to see that very movie last week (but lost the argument), now refuses to go along with his sister and holds out for yet a fourth movie. Discord! Anarchy! (But solvable!)

Last year we started a new practice that has kept the fighting down to a slow simmer instead of an ongoing boil. Each child writes one movie name on a piece of paper, and all drop their movie names into a paper bag. Then I stick my hand into the bag and pick a movie at random.

While their father stays home, catching up on weekend chores, I take the kids to the movies. Destination: whichever movie I picked out of the bag. Alternate choice: Any child who doesn't want to see that movie may stay home with Dad and catch up on homework or just play by himself/herself or read. But there is to be no fighting over the movie I choose from the bag.

Some weekends I wind up escorting one child to the movies while three stay home with Dad. Many weekends all four kids are with me, though, and usually there are at least two or three with me.

There is no way to please everyone. But this way the choice of movie is fair, and no one who doesn't want to see the movie is forced to sit through it. Anyone has the option of staying home . . . and missing out on the triple-dip ice cream cones we always stop off for after the movie.

Anonymous

Equal Opportunity Weekend Choices

Most weekends, we take our kids out for dinner and a movie, or occasionally lunch and a movie. From time to time they have other plans that preclude our usual movie-and-food, but it's a treat we all look forward to and generally manage to fit in somewhere between Friday evening and Sunday evening.

The kids used to fight over who gets to pick the movie. Sometimes I was ready to swear that one would say "No!" to a movie just because the other had chosen it. But three years ago we settled on a system that has cooled down the fighting.

If Jodi picks the movie, Tim gets to choose what restaurant we're eating in, and vice versa. And if this weekend Jodi picked the movie and Tim the restaurant, next weekend Tim picks the movie and Jodi the restaurant. Simple? Sublimely! So why didn't we think of this sooner?!

This actually is a throwback to a rule my mom had when I was a kid: Sunday nights she'd cook a treat of my choosing one week and a treat of my brother's choosing the next week. Whoever didn't choose the dinner got to pick what we watched on TV (we only had one set).

I guess you could say that our rule for weekend movies and restaurants is carrying on a family tradition, if an altered one!

By the way, when my son gets to choose the restaurant, it's usually the "Golden Arches" or some other fast food, and we get off cheap, but my daughter's tastes are both more eclectic and more extravagant. While she sometimes chooses Chuck E. Cheese or Burger King, it's as likely to be the local Chinese, or a family-style Italian restaurant (where she's partial to the veal parmigiana—ouch!), or the local fish restaurant (where she likes the batter-fried shrimp). I suppose I should be grateful she has a taste for something besides fast food . . . or, on the other hand, grateful she hasn't discovered lobster! But some of those dinners tend to run to a few dollars more than we'd hoped to spend.

Anyone reading this who wants to adopt our tradition but adapt it so it's less costly could offer the kids a choice of restaurants from among those on a list. The list would then contain only those that are affordable.

Anonymous

Fostering a Love of Good Writing

I've tried to raise my kids with an appreciation for the printed word and for a well-turned phrase. To foster this love of good or interesting writing, and respect for the power of words, I've started a new family bulletin board alongside the one for messages ("Mom, I'm at Chris's").

This one is strictly for well-put and interesting writing that the kids can relate to. We all contribute to it—the kids and I. (I'm divorced, so it's just the two of them, ages nine and twelve, and I.) They're encouraged to clip interesting short items they read if they make telling points or are well expressed. We don't always agree on what's telling or well expressed, but the rule is that it's everybody's bulletin board, and I don't veto any contribution unless it's in flat-out bad taste or some other kind of problem.

Comic strips have even shown up on the bulletin board on occasion, and why not? If a cartoonist makes a good point verbally (as opposed to pictorially), doesn't he or she deserve to have his/her work up on our bulletin board? But we've also had clippings from newspapers, magazines—even a fan magazine one of my kids bought. (And why not? The quote in question was a very well-put, one-paragraph description of a rock star's home, so well written that it definitely deserved a place on our bulletin board.)

As the board becomes cluttered, the oldest items are disposed of to make room for new ones.

My nine-year-old is already showing an interest in creative writing. If he grows up to pursue a literary career, that will be fine, but if he or his sister just grow up to be voracious readers—

and people who can write coherent business letters and personal letters that grab their addressees' attention—that will suit me fine too. It's not my stated aim to raise Pulitzer-winning journalists, just literate citizens with a good appreciation for the printed word and an equally good ability to express themselves verbally.

Anonymous

Sleep-overs with Sister

When my sister and I were kids, we had very little sibling rivalry. Ev is barely one year older than I am, and we were exceedingly close through childhood. In fact, I can honestly say she was my best friend.

Ev and I had separate bedrooms, but every Saturday night I'd "sleep over" in the extra bed in Ev's room. That bed was there for sleep-over guests, and when Mom put it in, she surely envisioned visiting friends as the prime users, but in actual practice I slept there more often than anyone else.

We'd make a big bowl of popcorn and eat it. Sometimes we played games, but often we'd just talk. Either way we'd stay up late, listening to records while we talked or played games. Mom was tolerant of the hours we kept. It wasn't a school night, and we weren't playing the music loudly. When we finally got in bed, we'd still keep talking till all hours.

This went on from early childhood right through till Ev went away to college, and when she came home on holiday breaks, I spent many of the nights she was home in the spare bed in her room.

Now we're both in our thirties. Ev's divorced; I'm married. Ev comes over to our house for the night with some frequency. Now she's the "sleep-over guest," staying with me, instead of vice-versa. Of course I don't spend the night in the guest room with her, but we do sit up till all hours in the living room or the guest room, gabbing. My husband knows not to wait up for me those nights. He knows I'll be late getting to bed.

I still enjoy sleep-overs with my sister. And I'd still say she's my best friend.   Anonymous

Liberal Sunday "Dining"

My mother was very strict about what we kids could and couldn't eat, and there was never any snacking between meals. She wouldn't let us spoil our appetites for dinner. But on Sundays, this all changed.

On Sundays, we would sort of be set free. We could eat anything we wanted to and snack all we wanted, because on Sunday evenings the meal was just popcorn and cheese, not a regular dinner like the other days of the week. We'd sit in front of the TV watching "Wonderful World of Disney" and snacking on popcorn and cheese.

I had a sister and brother, and all three of us Deming kids would proudly march around the house on Sundays saying, "We can eat anything—we can eat the piano!" It gave us a celebratory feeling.

David Deming
Chapel Hill, North Carolina

The Great Debates

Considering that my folks hated to hear my sister and brothers argue—and with four kids, there was a lot of arguing in that household!—I was surprised at first, back when I was around eleven, when they instituted Debate Night the first Sunday of each month. You never heard such arguing as went on then!

My parents would assign a topic to us. Sometimes it was on a kid level, like "Should school tests be abolished?" or "Should you let a friend copy your homework?" and other times—especially as we got older—it was on a more adult level, like "Should military service be strictly voluntary?" "Should the Welfare system be abolished?"

We were assigned sides, pro and con, a week before the debate, so we had time to prepare. Often we were assigned the opposite viewpoint from the one we personally held. I suspected then and still suspect now that that was deliberate. Our parents wanted to make better debaters and researchers out of us, I'm sure; I also believe that it was done to make us see the other person's point of view.

My mother admitted to us more than once that that was one of the reasons they instituted the debates: Debating, regardless of which side you took, gave you an opportunity to hear the other side to an argument. I suspect that by making us argue the point of view counter to what we believed, they were trying to get us to see even more clearly the other side's way of feeling and thinking.

And it worked. I think all four of us grew up quite tolerant and willing to listen to the opposing viewpoint in any discussion. We also learned at an early age to organize our thoughts.

And, because debating themes tied in to current events required reading the newspaper, or at least parts of it, we were better informed about the world around us than many of our peers.

But, because we threw ourselves spiritedly into anything we did—even defending a position we were personally opposed to—it sure got noisy around our house the first Sunday night of every month!

Anonymous

Family Gallery

≈++≈

With four kids, I don't have enough room on the fridge for the usual memos and notes *and* their best artwork. I long ago gave up on hanging their "masterpieces" in the time-honored location and instead gave over a long wall in our hallway to their artwork.

I covered one whole long hallway wall in corkboard, bought a package of pushpins, and made a sign that said, "The H_____ Family Gallery." To insure equal representation for each child, placement on the corkboard wall is not awarded by merit. Rather, each kid has the right to have three pictures hanging at any one time, pictures that he or she chooses. While I admit to sometimes trying to gently steer them toward hanging up one picture rather than another, the ultimate decision rests with each child.

The chosen artwork can be from school or home. And the medium is entirely up to the kids: we've had crayon drawings, finger-paintings, glitter-and-glue creations—you name it— gracing our family gallery. In fact, since my eleven-year-old got a camera, she's been hanging photos instead of drawing, a recent development in our tradition, but one I see no problem with. After all, photography is an art too.

When the kids were younger, they were mostly represented on the wall by pages torn from coloring books and by crayon or colored-pen scribbles. Never did we discourage them or say, "That's not good enough." Each child was and is entitled to three pictures on the wall at any given time, three pictures of his or her choosing, the three pictures he or she thought represented his/her current best—or maybe just his or her current favorites.

Family Customs and Traditions

Our ten-year-old, who has no special aptitude for art, is beginning to show a budding flair for writing. He wrote a short story for a school assignment that his father, his teacher, and I all thought was particularly good for his age. My husband and I are now debating whether to broaden the scope of the family "gallery" to include writing as well as art, and allow our ten-year-old to put up his writings in lieu of artwork.

We haven't yet come to a conclusion about this. We even considered corkboarding the opposite wall in the hallway and covering it with the kids' writings, though so far only one has shown any great flair in that field. We certainly want to encourage creativity of all kinds, however, regardless of how we ultimately decide to handle displaying his work.

Anonymous

Family Customs and Traditions

Snuggle and Tickle Time

For years my husband and I had a ritual with which we began our Sunday mornings with our two young sons. They'd be up at about 5:30, and we'd pretend we were sleeping throughout the murder and mayhem, but by 7:15 or so we couldn't pretend any longer. So we'd shout, "Snuggle time!" or "Tickle time," and the kids would come into our bed.

For a half an hour we'd have "snuggle and tickle time"—which also involved a great deal of shouting—and that's how we began every Sunday morning till the boys decided they'd grown out of it. The little one was five or six and the older boy eight when they decided they were beyond "snuggle and tickle time," but after we stopped, they both missed it.

Anonymous

Daddy's Own Bedtime Stories

In common with so many parents, I used to tell bedtime stories to our son when he was very little. However, parents were just beginning to recognize the negative aspects of fairy stories, and in any event such tales were not really part of our background.

So instead of the fairy tales, and since my son had long asked for a cat as a pet, I substituted a long series of stories about "Peter the Pussy." Peter had a different adventure each night, which I made up as I went along, and each of which led to a lesson for little children. Aesop in suburban New York!

Despite the fact that the stories were terribly moralistic, the kid loved them.

Anonymous

Dinner Discussions

Every night at the supper table, my children were allowed to discuss anything they wanted to. We didn't believe children should just sit there and eat and listen. This was our fun time, and it always turned out well.

I worked ten hours a day, but at dinner we all got together, and the children could ask anything they wanted to know about or discuss any topic they wanted to talk about. It was our special time.

Gracie Newsom
Benton, Tennessee

"Tell Me about When You Were Little"

Our son Joel is four and a half and has started a custom in our family called "Tell Me About When You Were Little." That's a question he asks frequently; then we have to dredge our memories for some story about our childhoods. He wants to hear all the stories my husband and I can think of, like the time my brother's friend put a frog or fish down my sister's back, or about the Indian tepees we used to make.

My husband has told Joel and Tyler stories about things he did with his grandfather, who was a farmer and used to take the cows to market. Grandpa "Slabs" (he got his nickname from being involved in lumber) is more real to them than most living relatives in our family, because they know him so well from all these stories their dad has told them.

It's a little wearing on the parents, because you have to stop and think. Memory is interesting. Sometimes a totally unrelated item will jog a memory: "Oooh, I haven't told my kids that." And I file it away in my mind so next time Joel says, "Tell me a story about when you were little," I have it to tell. Though they don't mind hearing the same stories over and over again, they do ask for something new every time.

Sherry Yeaton
Epsom, New Hampshire

Boxes of Poems

When I was a child, my mother kept a Whitman's Sampler box full of poems she had clipped from newspapers and magazines. As I reached maturity, I began clipping poems myself and storing them in a somewhat larger box, and as my children became old enough to read, I started a poetry box for each of them.

The children decorated their own poetry boxes. My older daughter covered hers with leftover wallpaper, glued on. My son cut out pictures of his cartoon heroes and pasted them on his box, and my youngest—a girl—crayoned the small cardboard box I gave her.

Into each of these boxes the kids put poems that appeal to them. I don't let it bother me if some of it is doggerel or tends more toward the limerick than to anything meaningful (or what would be meaningful to me, at least—obviously these poems *are* meaningful to the kids!). The important things are that the kids have an appreciation for poetry in some form and that they have the proprietary pleasure that comes from being able to choose their own poems for their own collections.

I never belittle or challenge their choices. I do sometimes say, "Why is this particular poem important (or meaningful) to you?" but if the answer is just, "I like it!" or "It's funny!" I absolutely accept that.

It's my hope that their tastes will grow and broaden as they grow older, but if any of them lose interest in poetry as they grow older, that's their right and privilege, and if this introduction to poetry leads not to an appreciation of lyric poetry but to a desire to become a rock lyricist, that's fine too.

Anonymous

Fudging the Endings

My family was very big on reading, and I was required by my parents to read one book a week over and above whatever I had to read for school. It could be fiction or nonfiction, on any topic I chose, but I was on my honor to read a book I had not read previously. Then every Friday night at dinner, I had to give an oral book report on that book.

I will confess that many weeks I didn't finish the book by Friday, and on those occasions I made up the ending when giving the book report. It didn't occur to me for years that one or both of my parents had probably read that book years ago, remembered it, and knew it didn't end as I said it had. I guess they must have felt I was learning fiction-writing by spinning out my own endings, and perhaps that was why they let me go on inventing endings for books, instead of lecturing me on veracity and honor.

I didn't grow up to be a fiction writer, however. I'm a teacher. And I'm very much on guard for students who turn in book reports with endings that don't match the originals. I've caught such happenings more than once or twice. My parents did succeed, however, in instilling a love of reading in me, and perhaps, after all, that's why they let me go on inventing book endings. I went on reading a book a week for years, often truly finishing them and giving accurate and honest reports.

And, inspired by my own past transgressions, I sometimes give my classes exercises in creative writing by asking them to rewrite the endings of famous books.

I also carried over my parents' book-reading requirements to my own two children, insisting they, too, read an extra book a week and report on it at the dinner table on Sundays. (I've changed the due date from Friday to Sunday so they have the weekend to frantically finish the book they've put off reading all week.)

So far, I haven't caught either of them fudging the endings.

Anonymous

Christmas and Chanukah
Celebrations

It came as no surprise that more of the contributions of traditions and customs for this book centered around Christmas than around any other single holiday. Christmas is probably more of a big deal than any other occasion, including even birthdays and Mother's Day.

Merchants certainly do their part to hype the holiday, but the people who contributed to this book demonstrated by their offerings that lots of people out there can see beyond the commercialism. While, for most kids, the main thrust of Christmas is waiting to see what Santa brings (and no one can deny that getting presents is fun even for adults), that's not all that Christmas is about.

Even beyond celebrating the religious event that was the genesis of the holiday, Christmas is also a time for giving as well as getting, a time for extra goodwill toward our fellow humans, a time for extended family get-togethers, and a time for doing what we can for those less fortunate than we are.

It's also, understandably, a time when many families have their own unique traditions and customs.

Christmas Codes: Guess Whose Package?

At Christmas, instead of my parents putting the names of my four brothers and me on our presents, they always create codes. They still do this, even now. Before we can claim our presents, we first have to figure out what belongs to whom by deciphering the codes, which vary from year to year.

My parents would always give hints in advance of Christmas, as to what this year's code was going to be, and by Christmas Eve we'd have figured it out. The codes were of different sorts every year.

One year, for instance, when we were all still young and living together, it was based on the phone book. It happens that where we grew up, there was at least one family with a last name that was the same as each of our first names. That is, my name is Gayle, and there was a family whose last name was Gayle; I have a brother Neal, and there was a family named Neal, and so on. That year the codes on the packages referred to page numbers in the local phone book. The code number on my packages referred to the page on which appeared the listing for the family named Gayle; on my brother Neal's packages was a code number that matched the phone book page on which there was a listing for a Neal, and so on.

Another year the code was the time of each of our births. For example, I was born at 10:45, so, omitting the colon, they coded all my packages 1045. My brothers' packages all had codes referring to their times of birth as well. Once we figured out what the code was based on, and because we all knew our birth times, we were able to figure out which presents were whose.

Family Customs and Traditions

Still other codes are alpha-numeric, with A equivalent to 1, B standing for 2, C for 3, and so on. One year the code was the sum of the numbers equating to the letters in each of our names. For instance, in my case, 7 for "G" + 1 for "A" + 25 for "Y" + 12 for "L" + 5 for "E". The letters' numerical equivalents added up to 50, so all my packages were coded 50 that year, and my brothers' packages all had numbers arrived at the same way, by adding up the letters in their names.

Another year, my parents added up the letters in our horoscope signs. And another Christmas, when we were all grown and living in different cities, they added up the letters in the city in which we were each living. One year the code was a map showing a city bearing each of our names—we were given a page in the atlas as a clue, and we had to find our names on that page in the atlas.

As we've each gotten married, our spouses have been included in the Christmas coded-package fun, so now our spouses have coded packages to decipher, too, and the tradition continues.

Gayle Keane
Citrus Heights, California

Christmas Is for Thinking about Others

We've tried to teach our children "The Christmas holiday is about other people, not yourself," and the way we celebrate it is in keeping with that belief. My husband is Muslim and doesn't celebrate the religious holiday, but we do have a seasonal celebration in the form of a huge open house on Christmas day.

We invite about 150 people every year; some are Jews or Muslims who don't celebrate the religious aspect of Christmas; others are widowed or are from other countries, and would be alone on the holiday if we didn't invite them to join us.

My two sons and I make everything for the occasion: decorations, food, and gifts. Everyone who attends gets a little homemade gift when they leave. It's a great tradition for the kids, and I'm amazed at the impact it's had on them.

Sandra Akacem
New London, New Hampshire

Christmas Shoeboxes

My friend Phyllis's family has an unusual replacement for stockings at Christmas. She has no idea how this custom got started, but instead of hanging stockings at the fireplace, the kids each put a shoebox under the tree. When they wake up on Christmas morning, their shoeboxes are outside their bedroom doors with presents in them.

Judith Zapadka
Oregon, Ohio

Around-the-World Christmas

I've been with the military and traveled quite a bit. Therefore, we don't have just one single Christmas tradition. Traveling from country to country, including Germany, Poland, England, France, Italy, Newfoundland, and Wales, we learned many other countries' Christmas traditions.

After we returned to the States, we began picking one country each Christmas and having the meal and other traditions that went with that country's Christmas holiday. As much as we could, we didn't go with just United States-printed cookbooks for the recipes but contacted people from that country to get their recipes and traditions.

Another Christmas tradition for us: We have two daughters, and we had the tradition of giving them each a new nightgown or slippers. They knew that at 9:00 or 10:00 at night, they could open one of their presents—usually their Christmas night-gowns, which they would wear that night.

They were both good about Christmas morning, waking up before us. They knew that opening the presents was a family affair but they could get at their Christmas stockings before we woke up, even in the wee hours. They waited for the rest of the family, though, before getting to the presents under the tree.

On Christmas, when the children were old enough, we alternated between them and us as to who would do the decorations around the house. We gave them access to different books so they could follow the customs of whatever country we were celebrating in the style of, that year. We picked the countries according to which one's customs we hadn't followed lately.

Jerry S. Kosowski
Little Rock, Arkansas

Christmas Cheer

My father has been decorating his house for Christmas for twenty-eight years. Each year, when he turns on the Christmas lights for the first time, he serves free food and beverages. The local church choir sings, and the Salvation Army is there to do a fund raiser. Everything is free.

He also places a mailbox on his lawn for kids to place letters in to Santa. He responds to all the letters. He does it because he loves people and is a big kid at heart.

Last year over 2,500 people showed up for the lighting party (that was in one night)! He plays Santa every night after work and gives toys, food, and clothing to the poor.

Killeen Quick
Port Jervis, New York

Impatient Christmas Eve

※+ +※

Christmas Eve has always been an incredibly long stretch of time for my impatient children. There seems to be nothing inventive or entertaining enough to do while they wait for what is clearly the big event—the arrival of Santa. Of course, for Santa to arrive, the children have to be in bed, asleep—difficult considering their high level of enthusiasm and unbridled joy. To give the entire family a way of settling into Christmas Eve, I began a tradition of buying and decorating the tree that evening.

After dinner we walk to the corner greenmarket, purchase the best of the trees—which are now selling for half the price they were going for a week ago—drag the tree home, and begin stringing the lights. Tree-decorating is always accompanied by popping corn, playing Christmas carols in the background, and reminiscing about Christmases past as we unwrap and hang each of the ornaments.

Another part of this tradition involves each family member giving the others a tree ornament, which can be opened on Christmas Eve and placed directly on the tree. We add these last and then, by the time all the decorations are up, the lights are on, and the caroling has begun to slow, the children are ready to take their baths and drop happily off to sleep, tired from the activity and ready at last for bed.

Irene Prokop
Summit, New Jersey

Family Customs and Traditions

"Jack Horner Pie"—Inedible but Fun

Every Christmas Night, our family enjoys a Jack Horner pie after dinner. It's not the kind of pie you eat, but it's definitely enjoyable. Though I don't know where this tradition originated, I can tell you that my husband's mother prepared one of these pies for him every year when he was a child; he's now sixty-seven, and we're still doing it at our house. His mother, who's now ninety-eight, has lived with us for the last six years, so she still gets to participate in these pies every Christmas. Here's what it's all about:

The "pie," which may be round or octagonal, actually contains gifts. It's made out of cardboard and tissue paper, and is about 15″ to 18″ in diameter, sometimes bigger if the gifts it contains are bigger. There's one small and inexpensive gift for each person present at dinner; the cost for each gift might be from $5 to $20. A string attached to each present leads to the recipient's place at the table and has his or her name on it.

Sometimes a Jack Horner pie gift is a little piece of inexpensive jewelry. My kids love reading, so they'll often each get a book, either a novel or some other book that, due to its author or topic, we know they'd love. Often they say, "This is just what I've been wanting to read."

My husband usually buys the gifts for the pie (except for his, which I buy), though this year I bought the pie gifts (except for mine, which he bought). Whoever attends Christmas dinner at our house gets a pie gift. My uncle attends every year, so he always gets a gift.

I suppose the pie got its name after the nursery rhyme character, but I have no idea how the tradition started.

When my present husband and I got married, my daughter and son (from my first marriage) were eleven and thirteen, respectively. My son celebrates Christmas Eve every year with his father and grandparents. He thought the tradition of the pie was so great he went out and bought gifts to give his father and grandparents, and made a Jack Horner pie to put them in.

The kids are now twenty and twenty-two, but we still carry on the tradition, and even now as adults they look forward to the Jack Horner pie.

The nicest part about this tradition is that even though there's a letdown on Christmas after the gifts are opened, with the Jack Horner pie to look forward to after the Christmas dinner dessert, the kids (and even the adults!) have something more to look forward to.

Karen North Wells
Brewster, Massachusetts

Ornament Exchange

My mother, who lives in Southern California, has a Christmas party every year at which our family gives each other ornaments with the name of the giver and the recipient, and the year. My mother, brothers, nieces, aunts, and uncles all take part in this. We hang the ornaments on the tree at my mother's when we get them, but then we take them home with us to keep, to put on our own trees in succeeding years.

My nieces are now little—one's three years old, and the other's an infant. By the time they're grown up and have moved out, they'll have lots of ornaments and will be able to start their own trees.

This all started with a friend who had a tree-trimming party every year. People went to those parties and brought their children; now those children are going to the same annual party and bringing their own children. It's wonderful, because people attending the party spend time looking through the tree for ornaments given twenty or thirty years ago.

I personally give ornaments to other people every year, as well as my family. They're gifts that people don't throw away but cherish for years to come.

Vicki L. Skinner
San Francisco, California

Nosey's Christmas Party

Though we have no children, our friends do, and we like to buy gifts for them. It can get very expensive, though, if the adults start feeling obligated to exchange presents as well. So the gifts to our friends' children are presented as gifts from Nosey P. McDigger—that's our dog!

Every Christmas, Nosey has a Christmas party and gives her friends—who are actually our friends' kids—their presents. This way the presents aren't coming from us, but from Nosey, and so our friends don't feel obligated to give us presents.

Only kids are invited as guests at Nosey's party. No dogs.

Laury Egan
Bethpage, New York

A Season for Learning about Others

I'm Jewish and my best friend is Christian. Our families are close—the kids as well as us parents. When Julia and her family celebrate Christmas, they always have us over. They do a Christmas dinner, which we are invited to, and a Christmas breakfast too, at which everyone exchanges presents—us included.

When my kids were little, Julia explained the meaning of Christmas to them, the story of Jesus of Nazareth, why Christmas is celebrated—the whole thing. It helped them understand some of the differences between our two religions.

On Chanukah, Julia and her family come to our house. They listen while I say the prayers over the menorah, and while my family and I sing the hymn. Then we all enjoy a traditional Chanukah dinner. (They especially love the *latkes* [potato pancakes].)

Afterwards, we all exchange presents. The traditional way is to give the kids one present for each of the eight nights of Chanukah, but my husband and I don't feel we have to be bound by that rule. The number of presents each child gets depends on such factors as whether we've spent lots of money on one big gift for that child that year, and how our family's finances are holding up that year. So, since we don't necessarily give eight gifts, the kids get all their presents the first night. We give presents to Julia's kids, too, just as Julia and her husband give our kids presents on Christmas.

I have explained the story of the Maccabees and the meaning of the Chanukah candles to Julia's kids.

Whatever other friends or family members join Julia's family for Christmas, and our family for Chanukah, from year to year, our two families always celebrate the two holidays together. I know two families whose kids will not grow up ignorant about and intolerant of people of other religions!

Anonymous

"Hot and Cold"

We celebrate Chanukah with a twist, in our family. In accordance with the standard tradition, our daughter gets a present for each of the eight nights of the holiday, but instead of our just giving them to her outright, we play "hot and cold."

Each day we hide a present while she's not looking, and that night, after we light the Chanukah candles, our daughter searches the house for her hidden present. We give her "hot" and "cold" clues as to whether she's getting closer to or farther away from where that night's present is hidden. It makes getting it all the more fun when she has to find it first.

Anonymous

Chili for Christmas

When I was a child, my mother always made chili on Christmas Eve. She'd put up a big pot of chili in the evening, and we'd eat it when we got home from midnight mass.

On Christmas morning, nobody would want to eat breakfast, so she'd make stollen, a sweet German bread made with candied fruit—citron and cherries. Anyone who came to watch the presents being opened would share the stollen with us.

My mother has passed on, but now I carry on the traditions, making chili for Christmas Eve and stollen for Christmas breakfast. It just isn't Christmas Eve without chili, or Christmas morning without stollen.

Jomil Mulvey
San Diego, California

Family Customs and Traditions

Sneaky Santa

My family (the Bollmans) came here from Germany near the turn of the century. I don't know whether the Christmas customs we practice come from the Old Country or not. My grandfather died about fifteen years ago, and I never got to ask him.

For some reason, when I was growing up, Santa didn't come down the chimney overnight. Instead, his method was to sneak up to the door Christmas Eve, while everyone inside was distracted by the ongoing festivities. He'd leave oodles of toys and other gifts at the front door, knock loudly, and then flee lest he be discovered.

When I asked my father about it, he said that's the way Santa came to our family since back when my grandfather was a lad in the early part of the century.

Rik Bollman
Las Vegas, Nevada

Chicken Jokes

Our family is big on joke gifts for Christmas, and my mom has a thing for ugly chickens, so she gets a lot of ugly chicken gifts every year as Christmas gifts. Not only the whole family but also friends participate in this.

One friend goes to Goodwill every year, looking for the ugliest item she can find with a chicken motif for my mother, and each year she tries to outdo what she did the year before. Mom has gotten chicken-shaped candles, ceramic chickens . . . one year she got a framed, needlepoint rooster festooned with sequins. (I actually liked that one myself, and I wound up keeping it!)

Shannon Joplin
Seattle, Washington

Family Customs and Traditions

Christmas Gathering

On Christmas Eve and Christmas morning, instead of having a big family gathering, we have a lot of friends over, mostly people who don't have family in the area. We have a big dinner, and some of the guests spend the night at our house. Of course my kids are there too.

Earlier we've drawn names, each adult getting the name of one other adult, for whom he or she has to buy a present; nobody knows who has whose name. Many of the presents we give are joke gifts, and one year, someone gave someone else coal in their stocking, because allegedly they'd been bad that year. This past year, my sister joking said she'd like a year's supply of deodorant, and somebody gave her just that—twelve kinds of deodorant in a large box.

We open each present one at a time, starting with the youngest (my kids) and continuing through whoever is the oldest.

The kids think Santa brought all the presents, even the adults' gifts—that is, except for what's brought by the "socks and underwear fairy." The socks and underwear fairy brings just that. Everybody gets some.

After all the presents are finally opened, which takes about five hours, we all sit down to brunch.

Shannon Joplin
Seattle, Washington

St. Nicholas Eve

Ｍy mother, who is of German descent, always celebrated St. Nicholas Eve with us, as I do now with my kids. It falls on December 5, and is rarely celebrated in America, although it probably still is celebrated in Germany.

Here's how we celebrate it in our family: First of all, the kids have to each clean and polish a shoe or boot so it's nice for St. Nicholas. Then they take a bath. While they're bathing, St. Nicholas comes to the house and fills their boots or shoes.

If they've been good, he fills them with candy and cookies, including German-style Christmas cookies, shaped like Santa, and sometimes a little book. (They get their big presents on Christmas.) Theoretically, if they've been bad they'll get their shoes filled with lumps of coal, but this has never happened in our family.

Each child gets a new pair of Christmas pajamas every year, either red-and-white or with Christmasy decorations on them. When they get out of the bathtub they put on their new pajamas and come out to see what St. Nicholas left them.

Then the kids go to bed. Now, each of my two sons has a miniature tabletop Christmas tree of his own, in their room, just as my sister and I did when we were kids. And on this tree each boy has his own ornaments, all of one theme.

For instance, mine was bells—all the ornaments on my own personal tree were bell-themed. My sister's ornaments all were bears. My older son, Anthony, has things with wheels like trains and cars, and Eli, the younger one, has sports-themed ornaments. The parents choose the theme, not the kids.

Anyhow, during the night, after the boys are asleep, St.

Nicholas makes a return visit to the house—that's twice in one night!—and brings each boy a new ornament for his tree. The ornaments all have the boy's name and the year on them. Every year the kids have one more ornament for their trees, and by the time they grow up and move out, they'll have twenty or more ornaments to take with them to their new home and hang on their big Christmas tree.

Shannon Joplin
Seattle, Washington

Putting the Baby in the Manger

The baby Jesus that goes with my parents' nativity scene is separate from the rest of the scene, and our family has traditionally left Jesus out of the manger scene till midnight, Christmas Eve. At that time the youngest child, which for many years now has been my brother Jeff (currently thirty-four), puts the baby into the manger.

We all live far from my parents these days, but we all make it home for Christmas, and Jeff still gets to put Jesus in the manger.

Gayle Keane
Citrus Heights, California

No Competition

Our family's Christmas tradition is that no one may come downstairs on Christmas morning without the rest of the family. This prevents competition to see who can get to the presents first. No one goes downstairs till we're all gathered together upstairs. Then we hold hands and all go down together and open our presents.

Sandy Post
West Palm Beach, Florida

Drawing Names

We come from a large family, and all the different branches get together at Christmastime. It's impossible for everyone in such a large family to buy presents for everyone else—it would just get too costly. So our solution is to draw names from a hat or bowl, the way some offices do for their Christmas parties. This takes place every year, at the end of the Christmas festivities, in advance of the next year's celebration.

Of course we all buy presents for our immediate families, but beyond that, each person is responsible for getting a present for one other relative, whose name he or she has picked out of the hat at the previous year's Christmas party. With a year to think about the person for whom you're buying the present, you can come up with something creative, and of course you can do your Christmas shopping for that person in March or August (or make it yourself, if you're a person who's into crafts). It makes for a festive celebration and yet eases the budget strain on all the members of our large clan.

Anonymous

Birthday Party for Jesus

A tradition we intend to start soon is one that friends of ours already have in their family. This couple, who have ten children, live at a Bible camp—a Christian conference center. Every year, a couple of weeks before Christmas, they have an afternoon Christmas celebration that they term a "birthday party for Jesus." They invite everyone they know. The activities are not a whole lot of games and stuff; it's more singing carols, reading the Bible stories about Jesus, and so forth. The focus is on Jesus.

So much about Christmas is so commercialized, but I think their celebration is really neat, and I intend to apply the same principles when I start the tradition in our family. I plan to make a birthday cake, complete with candles. (How many candles would you put on a birthday cake for Jesus?)

Sherry Yeaton
Epsom, New Hampshire

Santa on Christmas Eve

When we were younger, we lived in the country in Wisconsin. Our grandmother, who lived about an hour away in Oshkosh, would always come down on Christmas Eve and take us out for a drive to go see the Christmas lights and whatnot.

By the time we came home, Santa would have come to our house, and we'd get to open our gifts on Christmas Eve. We'd stay up till 1:00 or 2:00 or 3:00 in the morning, and have a good old time playing with them. It was kind of neat, staying up and seeing all the lights, then finding Santa had come while we were gone.

Often we'd fall asleep in the living room, and our parents would have to carry us upstairs to bed, but we'd be up again at the crack of dawn, going at it full tilt.

George G. Miller
Orem, Utah

Christmas Breakfast—Plus Gifts

The excitement of Christmas evening in our house is only surpassed by that of Christmas morning. Considering the high level of excitement, as well as the availability of goodies, it is virtually impossible in our house to get anyone to sit down at the breakfast table for something nourishing. So to get the children to start the day nutritiously, I invented a Christmas breakfast tradition that incorporates what they like best—opening gifts—with what they like least—sitting still at the table.

After attacking the presents under the tree, the children know that there is always a little something on the table—a new Christmas placemat, a bright red napkin, a new napkin holder in the spirit of the season, or perhaps a drinking cup shaped like Santa with a straw coming out of his hat. These things are only used on Christmas morning and are put away so they remain "special" throughout the year.

Because no parent likes to cook elaborate breakfasts on holidays, we often have toaster waffles, hot oatmeal from the microwave, bagels bought the night before, or cinnamon toast and fresh fruit. Most of these items can be prepared right at the table, and sitting together as a family and giving thanks for the bounty of the day is always a way to start the day on a spiritual as well as nutritional high note.

Irene Prokop
New York, New York

Family Customs and Traditions

Orange Juice for Christmas Breakfast

When I was growing up, we had an orange tree in the back yard. The first year, it had just one orange on it. We thought the perfect time to pick it would be Christmas morning, so we did, and shared it, splitting that orange seven ways (five kids, two parents).

That started a holiday tradition for us. Now we pick oranges off the tree every Christmas morning and all—parents, kids, grandkids—have freshly squeezed orange juice every Christmas morning. It's become one of our holiday traditions.

Gayle Keane
Citrus Heights, California

Pick One Present

When I was growing up, our family had a tradition that everyone could select one present per person to open Christmas Eve, saving the rest of the presents for Christmas Day. You know how kids are; we'd all say, "We want to open them all now." But we were told, "You have to pick just one." This was after the Christmas Eve meal, and we were all in our pajamas. We'd each open one present, picking the one that looked best to us, and save the rest for Christmas morning.

Michael Kilgore
Orlando, Florida

Christmas, Southern California Style

When we were growing up in southern California, we'd go surfing every Christmas morning as soon as we'd opened all our presents. We'd always get some new surfing apparatus for Christmas anyhow, and of course we had to test it out!

Before I was old enough to drive, Mom would take us, but once I had a driver's license, Mom stayed home and cooked, and I drove my brothers and myself to the beach.

Vicki L. Skinner
San Francisco, California

Saving Memories on Tape

Although my husband and I have only been married one year, he has an eleven-year-old daughter from his previous marriage who lives with us, and we have a five-month-old daughter as well. Every Christmas we videotape our Christmas celebration. This includes decorating the tree and opening the presents, as well as the Christmas Night celebration.

We plan to start creating titles for each individual year's tape and are looking now at what different things we can do each year to make that year's tape special.

Patricia Gray
Montz, Louisiana

The Chanukah Man

≈⊰ ⊱≈

We had a tradition in our family called the Chanukah Man. Now, in the Jewish celebration of Chanukah there's no traditional bearer of presents, even though giving presents is certainly part of the Chanukah festivities. But we had no jolly fat man named Santa giving out the presents the way the Christian kids had. The Chanukah Man was my family's unique way of dealing with that imbalance.

We had a Chanukah menorah but nothing like a Christmas tree, and we had no personified gift-bearer, no big, round, red-suited, jolly Santa who made it so cheerful for some people. So my family made up this "Chanukah Man," who allegedly came to our house the same way Santa came to the Christian households. One year—the year my aunt (yes!) played the part of the Chanukah Man, "he" even wore the same kind of red suit as Santa. My father, on the other hand, chose to wear a toga-style outfit for his guest appearances as the Chanukah Man.

For the first few years I was fooled. I didn't notice that Chanukah Man bore an odd resemblance to my father. Then one year my grandfather was chosen to play the part. When I was sitting on his lap I tugged at his beard. In a dramatic moment the beard came off, revealing my grandfather. I was shocked to find out that Chanukah Man was really a family member.

In later years, after my grandfather and father had died, and my younger cousins were born, I became the Chanukah Man. That lasted till there were no cousins young enough to warrant a Chanukah Man. But now I have a son of my own, and I think he's old enough that he should expect a visit from a red-suited, full-bearded gentleman next Chanukah. The Chanukah Man strikes again!

Mark Koesterich

Haverstraw, New York

Wine and Song

〜⊰⊱〜

My wife's heritage is German, and we have a Christmas tradition regarding making a Christmas wine known as Waldmeister, a German word meaning "king of the woods." This wine is only made and served at Christmas, and the tradition goes back in my wife's family at least as far as her great-grandfather.

I'm using the words "make the wine" loosely. What you actually do is steep an herb called sweet woodruff in Rhine wine, a German white wine. You take about six handfuls of the dried herb and let it steep about thirty to forty-five minutes, then strain the wine through a linen handkerchief, and mix about five or six additional bottles of Rhine wine with the essence. Then, to twelve cubes of sugar, you add just enough water to cover them, to make a simple syrup. Mix that into the wine mixture and add sufficient claret (a red wine) to give it a nice, deep, rosy color. Then rebottle it and chill it.

It can only be drunk at first at midnight on Christmas Eve, when the family gathers around the Christmas tree and sings "Oh Tannenbaum." From that point on, throughout the Christmas season, that wine is the traditional drink.

My wife's father always made this wine, and when I came into the family, I learned how to make it. I've been doing it now for almost fifty Christmases (my wife and I have been married for forty-seven years). We have four children and are passing the tradition down through the family. The problem is finding the sweet woodruff. We couldn't get it from our previous supplier this past year, and almost didn't have Christmas wine this year.

Owen Elliott
Juno Beach, Florida

Family Customs and Traditions

A Tradition-Filled Christmas

My family is of Irish-Catholic ancestry, so Christmas was very important to us in both the religious and the family sense. We had our set of traditions that we followed every year: The week before Christmas, we'd go out to the local nursery and buy a tree. My mom was very adamant about the tree configuration: very full (no bare spots), but not too tall. Thick and green. And a scotch pine was the only kind that would do.

We'd go out to dinner afterward, usually fast food. We'd eat in the car, and my dad would search the radio (AM) in the car, looking for Christmas music. (This was about 1960-1965, as I was born in 1956.) Then we'd take the tree home and start decorating.

My mom would give me, as the oldest in the family, the responsibility of decorating the inside of the house. I remember year after year resurrecting an old cardboard fireplace in our living room. You'd place a lightbulb in the bottom, and there was a spinner over it. The heat from the lightbulb would turn the spinner behind red waxed paper, which would give the illusion of a flickering flame. We would hang all our Christmas cards on this mock fireplace.

Christmas morning we'd open our presents, then spend all day playing with, or trying on, whatever we got.

The Christmas Day menu was always the same: Turkey, dressing, gravy, mashed potatoes, turnips, cranberry sauce, and mixed vegetables, with pumpkin pie for dessert. My grandparents would all be there.

Finally the night would wind down with my mom pulling out all the home movies and showing them on a bed sheet thumbtacked to the wall. At this point, all of us kids (one brother, two sisters, and I) were usually passed out on the floor, holding onto one of our new toys.

Jim Sutter
Boardman, Ohio

Large-Family Christmas

～+ +～

On Christmas Eve, after we go to church, we go back to my parents' house and get a whole spread of munchies, dips, chips, and lime sherbet punch. Then we all open our Christmas presents one by one. I am the youngest of five, and whoever can make it back that year joins in—usually about four of us—along with their children. At present my parents have ten grandchildren, and by the time this book is published, the count will be fourteen, with the ones currently on the way.

Santa comes with presents for the kids overnight, at their own houses, so they get them at home the next morning. The kids get their presents from their parents at the same time, but they get their presents from their grandparents and aunts and uncles the night before, at my parents' house, when the rest of us are exchanging presents.

Rochelle Mau
Olathe, Kansas

Family Customs and Traditions

Christmas Cookies

About two weeks before Christmas, my mother and I get together and bake. She does the cut-out cookies, and I do the decorating. We take great pains, using tweezers to spell out family members' names in sprinkles on the cookies. It takes hours. We pack up plates of cookies for each family—aunts, uncles, cousins—giving everyone an assortment of cookies on their plate.

When my son was little we put him in an apron, and he'd help out with the decorating too. Since he's gotten older, he hasn't kept up the interest, but I still get together with my mother and bake every year.

Robyne Gardner
Port Clinton, Ohio

Grab-bag Gift Choice

My parents had a variation on the eight-presents-for-Chanukah routine. Instead of arbitrarily choosing one present to give me on each of the eight nights, they tossed all eight gift-wrapped presents in a big pillowcase and allowed me to pick one present a night. Of course I had no idea what I was choosing. This gave a grab-bag atmosphere to the event and added to the general merriment more than if I were simply handed a present each evening.

Anonymous

Christmas Breakfast, Danish Style

✥

My great-great-grandparents came from a little village just out-side of Copenhagen, and our family has celebrated Christmas with a Danish Christmas breakfast for as long as I can remember. Everyone meets on Christmas morning at the oldest daughter's home, anytime between 8 AM and noon. For years, my mother was the hostess.

The menu consists of many dishes, most of them served cold, including roast goose stuffed with apples and parsley. The outside is rubbed with sugar so it's golden and crispy and sweet. We also have pork sausage and pressed lamb breast.

The lamb breast is layered with parsley, salt, and pepper, and rolled, then cut it in 6" slabs, tied, wrapped, and pressed in a meat press for about two months till it becomes about 1-1/2" high. It's excellent, one of my favorites. Other foods served at the breakfast include pork liver sausage and head cheese. All these meats are served cold.

The only hot dishes are kale and cabbage. They're cooked on pieces of pork in a large kettle, squeezed into softball-sized balls, and on Christmas morning, before they're served, they're put into a cast-iron frying pan with lard and heavy whipping cream, and heated till they're warm.

Then there's homemade bread, pumpernickel, rye, and white, sliced very thin. We also have about eight kinds of cheese: smoked edam, edam, brie, limburger, liederkranz, cream cheese, swiss, and cheddar.

And there are at least twenty different kinds of cookies. These include Danish sugar cookies. They're not really sweet; there's no sugar in the dough. But they're very rich and fattening, with butter and sugar on top. And "Berlin wreaths," which look almost like pretzels, and are tied in knots and decorated with meringue and red and green candied cherries. And spritz are another kind of cookies.

The thing my mom was most famous for was fruitcakes. The reason she was so famous for them is each was a year old. My mother started her Christmas baking in January. Each fruitcake weighed about five pounds and was about six inches in diameter. They were so rich, it was like eating a pudding. They were wrapped in gauze rags, and a cup of brandy was poured over each one once a month for a year.

On the Christmas tree there were special little cups made out of paper doilies; they looked like cones. Those were filled with candies and nuts and very small cookies, the stuff kids love.

Each place setting at the table had a water glass, a beer glass, a shot glass, and a coffee cup, most of which were filled on a constant basis. My mother's favorite wine for this occasion was cherry kijafa. It was only used for special occasions at our house, like my mother's birthday and Christmas.

Generally breakfast was served in shifts, adults first and children after. After breakfast the kids opened their presents. Grandma passed them out. The kids had to sit and wait for one present to be opened before another one would be passed out. Most of the presents were handmade. And then in the evening we'd all go to church. Then we all went home, tired and full, the cars packed with all the goodies Kris Kringle had left. Not Santa Claus—Kris Kringle.

Sue Schumacher
Lake Worth, Florida

Kids' Christmas Beliefs

These aren't actually traditions from my family, but I wanted to pass along some children's Christmas beliefs I've encountered in the course of my work. I'm a schoolteacher in Upper Manhattan, teaching kids from poor homes. Some of the holiday stories I hear from them are enough to give you a day's worth of laughter, and some could break your heart.

One of the funny ones I heard from a variety of different kids in my class last year was that Santa Claus got rid of his reindeer and now delivers all his presents by subway.

Another boy told me that his father had told him the Rudolph story, "but he can't fool me about that flying reindeer! I know it's not true! It wasn't his nose; it was a red lightbulb!"

On a more serious note, another kid told me of a conversation his father had had with him. His dad told him he'd talked to Santa. Santa, the father said, had asked if the family would be willing to do without presents that year, so a really needy family could get their presents instead, a family who would otherwise not get any presents. "But," the kid confided in me, "I know it's really that we just can't afford to get any presents ourselves."

Mark Koesterich
Haverstraw, New York

Personalized Ornaments for Nieces

We're really big into Christmas. One thing I started doing long ago with my nieces was to give them special Christmas ornaments every year. These ornaments would either have their names on them, or say "Niece," or have something on them to do with their birthdays. Each year each niece would get at least one ornament, sometimes more.

This has been going on since they were babies, and they're now fourteen and sixteen. When they're old enough to leave home, they'll have enough ornaments for their own trees.

Their mother's tree, of course, will then be naked!

Laury Egan
Bethpage, New York

Computerized, Customized Cards

We stopped buying commercial Christmas cards the year after we got our computer, which was five years ago. Now we make up our own Christmas cards on the computer, complete with a picture on the front (OK, it's black-and-white, but it's home-made, which gives it a certain charm), and a customized message inside.

I start out with a generalized message suitable to everyone. It varies from year to year but is generally along the lines of wishing peace and joy this holiday season and throughout the year. But then I write something special for the person or family the card is going to. When I see the quantity of pre-imprinted cards we get, with even the signature printed on, not signed/personalized, I'm proud of our cards and feel the hours I spend at the computer every pre-Christmas are justified. Our Christmas card list hovers around thirty in number—relatives, friends, and neighbors—but it's worth the time I put in on the computer, knowing we're sending out cards I truly can feel good about. The kids help with folding the cards after the computer spits out the 8.5" x 11" sheets, and with addressing, stamping, and sealing. Last year my son even asked for—and got—some input into the messages going to a few family members and friends. It has become a family project.

Anonymous

Family Customs and Traditions

Other Holidays, Birthdays, and Other Celebrations

Christmas may get the most attention in the calendar, but even though it gets the most attention on TV and in newspapers, in commercials and department-store decorations, and on the radio (when's the last time you heard a song commemorating Father's Day?), it's not the only holiday on the calendar.

Thanksgiving comes in for a fair share of attention, although I suspect a lot of that has to do with Thanksgiving being the official opening of the Christmas Season. I've lately been on a crusade to "Put the Thanks Back in Thanksgiving." Reading some of the contributions in this section, I'm heartened to know there are families out there in which the kids know Thanksgiving means something more than just three days off school, preceded by a week of enforced study about the Pilgrims.

We've even got Flag Day contributions here. (When was the last time you did anything meaningful for Flag Day? And I'm just as guilty!)

Also in this section are special celebrations for birthdays, those personal holidays that signal another year added to our individual histories and the start of yet another year, one that, as always, is bound to be full of unexpected events. (And, unlike a novel, you can't peek at the last page to see how it comes out.)

Birthdays have always been special to kids, but nowhere is it written that adults can't celebrate birthdays just as joyfully. Whether it's dinner in bed (one of the entries below) or some other form of celebration, adults can find a means to make their birthdays special too—even if you can't blow out all those candles with one breath. And as for kids . . . well, for most kids, their birthdays are the highlight of the year, often equaling if not topping Christmas.

What's *your* favorite holiday? And your favorite way of celebrating?

Sing for Joy

Our whole family, and I mean the extended family, is blessed with a talent for singing. On all holidays—not just Christmas—we go around and sing in nursing homes, in malls, in hospitals, and in nursery schools.

We think this brings a lot more happiness to people than a gift, an Easter basket, or a bag full of candy.

This tradition in our family was started a long time ago, before I was born. It makes me happy to do this, and we all have a lot of fun.

Jaime
Fairport, New York

Burning the Bad

The church we belonged to where we used to live had a really neat tradition that we've adapted and adopted for our own.

Our family has never done much with New Year's Resolutions. I find most people don't hold to them anyhow. But we do have the Burning of the Bad, as adapted from what our church used to do. On New Year's Day, we each write down the habits, traits, and attitudes we feel we need to get rid of. It could be a bad habit like chewing with one's mouth open, a trait like laziness, an attitude such as negativity, or anything else we recognize we need to stop doing/feeling/being. We write each individual item on a separate piece of paper.

Then we light a fire in the fireplace and gather around. We adults start (to set a good example), reading each sheet of paper aloud before tossing it into the fire. The kids follow us, from oldest to youngest (we have three kids). As we burn each piece of paper, we are symbolically getting rid of the habit or trait itself . . . and we make an effort to do just that in the days and months ahead.

Is it effective? Well, certainly not 100%, but do you know anyone who keeps all his/her New Year's resolutions? I honestly do feel that the symbolism of throwing the paper in the fire helps make the intent more real and raises our rate of success.

Anonymous

A Reason to Give Thanks

We didn't have any extended family living near enough to join us for Thanksgiving, but that doesn't mean it was just us five at dinner. My mom always invited a few people over who otherwise wouldn't have had much of a holiday.

Some years she "borrowed" two or three of the more spry and cogent residents of a local nursing home, folks who couldn't live alone anymore but were still able to sit at table with us and carry on a conversation. Some years she invited people who hadn't enough money to get a turkey and all the fixings for themselves, and would otherwise have had a bleak and cheerless holiday. One year the guest list included a friend of hers whose husband and only child had just been killed in a car crash, and who otherwise might have been alone for the holiday.

Some of the seniors who joined us told marvelous stories about Thanksgiving in the "olden days." My brother, sister, and I sat enthralled by some of the tales they told.

The poverty-level folks were a revelation too; I had picked up some negative attitudes about poor people, from some of the other kids in school, but the Thanksgiving dinners we shared with these people made me see these were just people like us, except they'd unfortunately had some bad breaks.

While our guests' plight was never mentioned in front of them, Mom always made sure we kids understood beforehand what their situation was, whether it was poverty, age, loneliness, or a physical disability. This was partly so we wouldn't make an unfortunate and painful remark in front of our guests, but also so that we would be appreciative of all the blessings we had.

Family Customs and Traditions

My mom's idea was not only to make Thanksgiving more meaningful for our guests, who otherwise wouldn't have had much of a holiday, but also to bring home a lesson to us kids and make us realize how much we had to be thankful for on this holiday (and every day).

Anonymous

Flag-Waving Flag Day

Nobody else in our community did anything for Flag Day other than a few families putting flags out front of their houses, but my dad had a different idea. He had fought for our country in Korea, and he was proud to be an American. He was determined to instill that same pride in all of us.

So on Flag Day we not only hung out the flag, we were all present when my dad put it up, and we saluted it, reciting the Pledge of Allegiance, after which we sang every patriotic anthem we could think of: not just our national anthem but "America," "America the Beautiful," and anything else that any of us knew. And we sang all the verses, not just the better-known first verses.

That evening the family gathered for a sing-along that featured such songs as "It's a Long Way to Tipperary," "The Marines' Hymn," "You're a Grand Old Flag," "The Battle Hymn of the Republic," "This Is My Country," "Anchors Aweigh," "Yankee Doodle," "I'm a Yankee Doodle Dandy," and other songs that are in some way either patriotic or singularly American.

I suppose both of us kids went through a phase in which the sing-alongs struck us as terribly corny, but we outgrew that phase and reverted to appreciating the patriotism our dad was instilling in us, and the family togetherness that was as much a facet of the celebration as was the patriotism.

Anonymous

Loving Hands Giftwrap

When my kids were old enough to understand what birthdays, Mother's Day, and Father's Day were, but not old enough to have money of their own to buy gifts with, I elicited their participation in a different but very meaningful way: I had them make the giftwrap for their grandmas' and grandpas' presents in a way that made the wrap uniquely theirs.

Spreading long sheets of brown paper out, I had the kids wash and dry their hands carefully while I filled a bowl of red fingerpaint and a bowl of yellow. Then I had my son carefully dip his hands in the red paint and my daughter do the same in the yellow. Then they shook the excess off their hands.

Each put his or her handprints in various spots on the brown paper, which made it very special to both sets of grandparents, more special than the present. The present came from me and was store-bought, as opposed to the wrapping paper, which came from the kids and was homemade and from the heart.

For a few years after the kids got an allowance and were able to buy their grandparents presents, they continued making the wrapping paper to wrap their gifts. When finally they decided they were too old to continue, both grandmas were regretful, one expressing the opinion that the (literally) handmade giftwrap was more precious to her than the present inside.

Anonymous

Two Birthdays Every Year

Our two daughters are adopted, and every year each of them celebrates two birthdays, her "B" birthday and her "A" birthday. Her "B" birthday is the day she was born; her "A" birthday is the day she was adopted. Both are equally important. Both merit presents. Both merit cards. Both merit a party.

In this way we have reinforced the positive side of adoption. Far from hiding their adoptions from our daughters, we have told them, from as early as they could possibly understand the concept, that they were "chosen." (Both were adopted when very young, the one at just over age four months and the other at not quite nine months.) And because these adoptions were important and joyous occasions for us, they call for celebrations.

With all the celebrating, both girls feel adoption is a good thing, and in fact the younger one feels sorry for all her friends who were "only borned, not adopted like me."

I can't imagine either girl will ever feel like she doesn't really belong in our family, is any less a family member for not being born into it, or is in any way inferior or lesser. We've always told them that the day each of them was adopted was one of the most important days in our lives—and we mean what we say wholeheartedly. But for the girls, the party each gets on her "A" birthday, and the presents and cards that go with it, are visible, tangible proof of the importance and joyousness of the occasion.

Anonymous

Thanksgiving Year-by-Year

=⧣+⧢=

You know the way some people collect one new Christmas ornament every year? Well, our family collects Thanksgiving ornaments—some of them homemade, some bought—one for each year. The oldest of them date back nearly twenty years.

Ornaments include a miniature "turkey," a plaster cornucopia (painstakingly painted), two hand-decorated pine cones, a lovely fall-themed wreath (the wreath is made of twigs, and there are a few artificial autumn leaves attached), and various other fall-themed or Thanksgiving-themed decorations.

Our family has memories attached to most of them. One is from the year we invited some new-to-America neighbors to join us for their first Thanksgiving. One is from the year we bought the Christmas tree the day before Thanksgiving, when the first load of trees went on sale in the neighborhood, and everyone teased us for getting into the Christmas spirit too early. One is from the first Christmas our son was away at college and couldn't be with us. One is from the "kitchen disaster year" (of which I won't give details!). And so on. The ornaments evoke memories both sad and sweet, and they all come out of storage a couple of weeks before the holiday.

I put them all around the house in appropriate places: On bookshelves, on shelves, on top of furniture, on the dining room table—wherever I find a suitable place. The ornaments don't all get put in the same places every year, except for the wreath, of course, which always goes on the kitchen door, since more people use that entrance than the front.

Our two kids each have their favorites among the ornaments. Predictably, our daughter's is one she made herself and our son's is one given him by his elementary school best friend, who moved out of state at the start of junior high.

We leave them in place right through the Christmas season, except for the wreath, which gets displaced; we move it to the front door, to make room on the kitchen door for our Christmas wreath. We always reminisce when we take out the ornaments and put them up. When we put them away again, it's with some measure of sadness. January 2 seems such an empty day, the end of a festive, holiday, good-will period, which always leaves me feeling sad and mildly depressed. But now that I'm in my late forties, I find the days and months go by quicker than ever, and I console myself with the thought that it'll be Thanksgiving again before I know it!

Anonymous

Annual Ornament on Baptism Day

⟞+ +⟝

My godmother gives me a Christmas ornament on my baptism day every year, as she has since I was one year old. Every year when my day comes, she comes over with a small bulb orna-ment, usually a Precious Moments. It always says "Godchild" on it.

She explained to me once that the reason for her doing this was so I'd always have something to remember her by, and also so I'd have a tradition to pass on to my godchild one day.

Every year we get out a miniature tree and hang just my spe-cial "godchild" ornaments on it. It makes me happy that my aunt/godmother cares so much.

Dawn Klemish
Saginaw, Michigan

Family Customs and Traditions

Remembering Mom on Kids' Birthdays

My husband taught our children to give me flowers on *their* birthdays, as a thank you. These special rewards for me on their birthdays seemed to fill in the gaps, make up for all the appreciation forgotten for the little things one does for the family. It's not a cover-all, but it does help.

It's a custom that I find happening in other families we associate with more and more often. The husbands seem to like the idea of remembering to thank Mom.

So many times, moms are not thanked for the myriad things they do. I only hope that my children (who are now about to get married) will teach their children this custom.

Renee Solomon
Toledo, Ohio

Holiday Baskets for the Homebound

To give Thanksgiving its true meaning for our two kids, we have for about six years now been taking Thanksgiving baskets to homebound people without families. Everybody has to contribute something—I do the cooking, my daughter helps, and my son makes decorations. My husband drives the baskets to their recipients.

When my daughter was younger, her contribution, like my

son's, was making decorations. These have included colored doilies, construction-paper Thanksgiving scenes, and the like. Additionally, this year my son volunteered to buy bubble gum out of his own money to put in some of the baskets. (I'm not sure how appropriate a choice bubble gum was, but I didn't want to discourage him from what was essentially a nice thought—spending his own money to put something "fun" in the baskets. So they went out with bubble gum in them.)

Most of the recipients are either temporarily ill or permanently disabled, though some are senior citizens who no longer drive. All are people who are shut in, have no family nearby, don't cook much, and wouldn't have much of a Thanksgiving if someone didn't lend a hand.

We make the arrangements ahead of time, either through our church or through a local charity. Then, Thanksgiving morning, I cook an extra turkey for these people, along with some simple side dishes, load up a basket for each (we feed from four to eight people, average, each Thanksgiving), make sure the kids' decorations are tucked into the baskets, and give them to my husband for delivery.

Anonymous

A Trip to Make You Thankful

Our family's Thanksgiving tradition when I was a child was to take a week's trip somewhere within one day's driving distance (or one year we flew to the Grand Canyon), to see a part of the country we two kids (and sometimes our parents) weren't familiar with. My parents felt that seeing different parts of our country would make us prouder of being Americans, and more thankful for this country we live in.

Family Customs and Traditions

We didn't have any other relatives in our part of the country (the Northeast), and my mother found early on that their friends were all busy with their own families and couldn't join us for Thanksgiving dinner. She hated to have Thanksgiving dinner for only the four of us, a night like any other (except we would stuff ourselves). That didn't feel very "holiday-ish" to her. So she and my dad decided to do something to celebrate the holiday in a way that would bring home the concept of giving thanks more clearly and make us realize how much we had to be thankful for.

That year we took a trip to Washington D.C. over Thanksgiving weekend. Other years we took full-week trips, with Mom and Dad letting me skip school on Monday and Tuesday of Thanksgiving week. (Believe me, I gave thanks for that, although I don't think it's quite what my parents had in mind!)

Not all our trips were to historic sites. Although we did go to Colonial Williamsburg and the Amish country of Pennsylvania, we also traveled to various sites around the country where we could see ordinary people like us, who lived in different surroundings. (For instance, we lived in a city; some of our trips were to rural areas.) One year we visited pockets of poverty just because our parents decided my brother and I weren't grateful enough for all we had, and we ought to see how some truly poor people lived. Though the effects were short-lived, my mom was right in assuming we'd learn a lesson from what we saw. We did a lot less begging that Christmas, and a lot less grousing about all the toys we didn't get.

By the following year, I'm afraid we were back to the buy-me buy-me syndrome. But still I have to say that, overall, the message we were supposed to get from these trips did sink in, and we did realize how lucky we were not only to live in this great country but to live in comfort and not want for the necessities.

Anonymous

"Color-me" Resolutions

Around our house, we don't believe in New Year's Resolutions as solely a tradition; we want them to be something more meaningful. We want them not just to be made but to be kept. I know all too many people who say, "I resolve I'll stop smoking," or "This year I'm going to pay more attention to my wife," or "I promise myself to read a book a week," or whatever good intentions they have—only to break every resolution by the second week in January.

Kids, too, take resolutions lightly. They make a resolution at their parents' prompting, then forget about it, possibly because they see their parents doing the same, possibly just because kids will be kids.

Well, not in this household.

My husband and I limit ourselves to two resolutions a year, and we do our darnedest to keep them. If we fail, we fail trying, not through being negligent, not caring, not bothering. Because our kids are old enough to understand what a promise is, we've asked them to make two promises to themselves and us every New Year's Day about things they're going to improve in themselves during the year ahead.

To enforce the resolution, we have them draw a picture of it. When they were too young to draw, my husband or I would try our best shot to draw the pictures ourselves, then ask the kids simply to color them.

We've drawn pictures of our son writing out his alphabet, pictures of our daughter tidying her room, and a really cute one of a unisex-looking grown person with his or her mouth open and a boy with a zipper over his lips, reminding our son to stop interrupting conversations. The appropriate child was asked to color in the picture, and was then asked to put the picture up on his or her wall as a reminder through the year.

Now that they're older, they draw their own pictures. Neither has a speck of talent at art, but that's not the point. The pictures were never intended to be entered in a juried art exhibition. They're re-enforcements, reminders, gentle guides to keeping those New Year's Resolutions.

On New Year's Eve every year we take the old pictures down from the walls, discuss with our kids how well they've done in keeping their resolutions, praise them wherever possible, and help them come up with two resolutions apiece for the next year. The resolutions have to be in areas where the kids genuinely need improvement, yet they have to be realistic as well. We don't want them setting such high goals that they're unattainable. Lofty intentions are wonderful, but we don't want the kids setting themselves up for failure.

By coloring in the drawings when they were younger, and now doing all the drawing themselves, they get a more meaningful grasp of the resolution. The intention is brought home to them. And the pictures, posted on their walls, serve as a frequent reminder, one we're not afraid to use by pointing them out ourselves and giving the kids an accompanying gentle verbal reminder when necessary.

Anonymous

New Year's Family Fun Night

In too many families, New Year's Eve is an excuse for the parents to go out partying, often coming home drunk on roads already full of drivers "under the influence," while the kids are left home with a babysitter who's getting triple-time pay for sitting on New Year's Eve.

Not in our house.

In our house we celebrate as a family. The kids get "punch" made of fruit juice mixed with ginger ale. My husband and I buy a very small, inexpensive bottle of champagne and have one drink each at midnight. (We believe it's healthy for the kids to see us having a drink in a responsible manner on an appropriate occasion. They're going to be exposed to alcohol as they get older. We're not teetotalers and don't expect them to be. But we do expect them to do their drinking responsibly and in moderation when they're old enough, and we're setting a good example for that right now.)

The kids are allowed to stay up till well past midnight—it's a special occasion, after all—and we make lots of noise when the clock chimes midnight. Some of it is with various kinds of homemade noisemakers the kids have a good time making for several days in advance.

Shortly before midnight, we all put on silly hats. Some years these have been store-bought and some years we've made our own, according to how silly the kids have felt that year.

New Year's Day is a day for making resolutions; New Year's Eve is a night for making merry. Since the theme of New Year's Eve is "ring out the old, ring in the new," we have several activities we usually engage in during the evening. One is a discus-

Family Customs and Traditions

sion of what we hope for in the New Year—it's a time for making wishes, however extravagant. (When appropriate, this is followed up the next day by a discussion on how to make the more practical of those wishes come true.)

Another thing we do on New Year's Eve, in connection with "ring out the old," is to look at home videos we've taken during the past year. One year the kids asked if my husband and I had any videos from our childhoods! We explained that home videos didn't exist in those days, but we dragged out the old 8mm projector and showed selected home movies from our childhoods. The kids weren't bored at all—they thought it was a hoot to see movies of Mommy and Daddy as kids! We've repeated that activity several years since.

A related activity, one year, was to show old cartoons that we'd bought on videotape. The kids know some of the cartoon characters of our childhood—Bugs Bunny and Daffy were around then, of course. But we showed them cartoons that even predated our childhoods, some old "Popeye" and "Betty Boop" episodes, and some "Looney Tunes" from the '30s and '40s.

Another family activity we enjoy on New Year's Eve is to cuddle on the couch and talk about "Favorite Moments." They don't have to be from just the past year, although we do put an emphasis on the year just ending. They could be from any time, as long as they're treasured memories . . . of something meaningful, something silly, something special in some way.

We don't eat a proper dinner on New Year's Eve. By the kids' request, we grill hot dogs in the fireplace, and later in the evening we make "s'mores" and pop corn. After all, it's a party night, right?

One year, after my husband had cooked the hot dogs over the fire and we'd made the s'mores, the kids decided it felt like a camping trip and asked for permission to sleep on the living room floor that night. Then they got the idea for us to join them there! After a few minutes' hesitation, we agreed, and the four of us spent the night in improvised bedrolls on the living room floor. The kids loved it, although my husband and I woke up achy and stiff in the morning. Still, it was fun, and we didn't regret it.

One year, the kids asked for party games, and we played Pin the Tail as well a couple of word games appropriate to the kids' ages at the time. The next year we were all caught up in home movies most of the evening, but the following two years we did games again.

The point is that, whatever we do, we do it together. It's a great way to start the New Year. Soon enough the kids will be wanting to go out with their friends on New Year's Eve. And we'll let them. But while they're still young enough, we want to make New Year's Eve a meaningful night for them, and at the same time set a good example for them.

Anonymous

Melodious Birthday

For everybody's birthday in my family, we always call and sing Happy Birthday to the person at work, then call their home and leave the song on their answering machine as well. When they get home, they find a bunch of birthday messages. It's a great thing for them to hear! I've started doing this for my friends on their birthdays, as well.

Vicki L. Skinner
San Francisco, California

Queen for a Day

There was a TV show in the '50s—before my time—called "Queen For a Day." Though I never saw the show, I thought the concept of treating someone like a queen for a day was great, especially if we could apply it to our mom. I was perhaps fifteen when I got this idea, and my brother would then have been fourteen.

At first we did this on Mother's Day, because it seemed fitting. But it bothered me that she was sharing the day with mothers all over the U.S.A. I wanted it to be just her day. So finally I decided to make her a queen on her birthday.

I asked Mom to take the day off on her birthday, and my brother and I cut school (with Mom's knowledge and consent, although it was given reluctantly that first year). Our dad didn't live with us; he and Mom were divorced when we were little kids. So he wasn't involved in the celebration.

Mom slept in that morning, and Tim and I made breakfast for her—a special breakfast. We would have served her breakfast in bed, but she doesn't care much for that, so we decorated the dining room with streamers and paper chains, and a big cut-out sign that said MOM = QUEEN. YOUR DAY. ENJOY IT. We bought a bouquet of flowers and put it in a nice vase, making it the centerpiece of the table. We made it a point to eat before she came downstairs, so she wouldn't have to spend breakfast reprimanding us for our table manners, cautioning us against eating too fast, or listening to us bicker. (We made a concerted effort to behave extra-nice to each other that day.)

We cooked breakfast for her, served it to her, cleared the plates afterward, and washed and dried and put away the dishes. Then I ran a bubble bath for her, even though she'd had a shower the night before. She went back upstairs, bathed luxuriously, dressed, and came back downstairs.

We spent part of the morning telling her why she's a special mom to us and sharing some of our favorite childhood memories with her. About a half hour into this, she said she wished she were taking notes, so we got out the cassette recorder, put in a blank tape with another nearby to pop in if the first one ran out, and started over. When we were done with our recollections, she came up with some memories of her own of our childhoods. Some we had heard before; much of it we hadn't. We listened raptly. She now has the whole thing on tape, our memories and hers, and all the laughter (and yes, some tears too).

After that, I went into the kitchen and started preparing a scrumptious lunch, while Tim set the table again, using the good china and silver. Mom was impressed—she didn't think I could cook anything that elaborate. (To tell the truth, I remember being surprised, myself, that it came out all right.) We all ate together—Tim and I on our best behavior—and then we presented Mom with a book we'd bought for her and told her to curl up on the couch with it while we cleaned up. We both cleared the table, and then, because I'd cooked, Tim did the dishes.

Mom read for several hours while Tim and I cleaned the house, a chore that we always helped with but that normally fell mostly to Mom. Then we hopped a ride to the supermarket with our neighbor—prearranged—and did a massive shopping, so Mom wouldn't have to. (She gave us the money for it, of course, but we relieved her of the burden of doing the actual shopping, which she otherwise would have had to do that weekend.)

My mom only drinks on special occasions, and we decided this was one of them, so when we got the groceries put away— it was around 4:30 by then, if I remember right—we poured her a glass of wine and sat with her in the living room. She began to reminisce about her childhood birthdays, and Tim and I heard stories we'd never heard before. We were fascinated.

Then we all dressed up and went out for dinner, to someplace modestly price that Tim and I could afford on our saved-up allowance, and we treated Mom. It wasn't elegant—elegant wasn't in our budget—but it was a night out, and our treat, and there were tears in Mom's eyes when we paid the check.

We asked Mom how she wanted to spend the evening—we had nothing special planned—and she suggested that we'd spent enough time with her and might want to be with our friends. (I had earlier cut short a phone call from my best friend, saying, "I can't talk to you; it's my mom's birthday and we're celebrating all day," which touched Mom deeply, she said.) But we told her we could see our friends 364 days a year; this was her day.

Mom's a great gardener. Because her birthday falls in early June, and we'd had dinner fairly early, it was still light out, and she went out to work in her garden. We wouldn't dream of telling her not to work in the garden on her birthday—working in the garden isn't like real work to Mom—but we did go out and help her, after we all changed clothes to something appropriate for gardening. We spent a lovely hour together till it got too dark to work; then we all sat out in the yard and talked. Then it was time to go in, since Tim and I both had school the next day.

The dinner had taken a big bite out of our piggybanks, so that and the book were the only gifts we gave Mom, but she was in ecstasies over the wonderful birthday, and we resolved right then to do it again the next year . . . and we did.

I'm twenty-five now, but every year Mom takes off work on her birthday, and Tim and I take off from whatever we would otherwise be doing (work, for both of us, these days) to spend the whole day with her. The first few years, the program was pretty similar to that first year, but we've had wide variations since then as we got driver's licenses, as we got incomes and were able to treat her more lavishly, and as we got better ideas as we got older.

We've taken Mom to lavish dinners, on picnics, to concerts, and to a museum. We've cooked truly fancy dinners at her home—Tim's become quite a decent cook too!—and we've invited friends in to help celebrate, doing all the preparations and the clean-up ourselves. But we still clean the house for her (although neither of us lives there anymore, and the place is much cleaner to start with!), still go shopping at the supermarket for her, still pamper her and fuss over her and don't let her do any work on "her" day—except in the garden—and still spend a good deal of time reminiscing, and devote at least some time to telling her just why she's a special mom.

It's her day, she's "queen for a day," and she loves it.

Anonymous

Special-Occasion Choo-Choo

Our tradition started with the gift of an electric train, ten years ago at Christmas, to our firstborn. I thought his grandparents were purely nuts to give an electric train to a child so young, but they said, "He'll grow into it, and there'll be other kids. It's for all of them. Wait. Fifteen years from now they'll all still be playing with it."

Thirteen years (and one more child) later, it looks like they were on the right track (pun intended), although they had no idea of the tradition that would grow around their gift.

When Milo was a year old, we set up the train set, arranged it so the tracks went around behind a chair, and put Milo on the floor nearby. While I kept Milo busy, his dad, over behind the chair, put a small toy on the train as it ran past the chair. When it reached Milo, I stopped the train so it could "deliver" Milo's gift. He was delighted!

When Milo was two, none of his gifts were small enough to fit on the train. But I wrote a note that his dad—hiding behind the chair again—put on the train that said, "Look under your bed and find a birthday present." I showed Milo the note as it came around on the train, read it, and escorted him back upstairs to search under the bed, where he found the present. (And where I found an old banana skin . . . but that, as they say, is another story.)

Since then, we've hidden all the presents every birthday and Christmas. We set up the train the day before and write notes directing the kids to the presents. On the big day, my husband hides behind the chair and puts the clue notes in the train one at a time as it chugs past him. Then the birthday child (or Christmas gift recipient) removes the note, reading the clue as to where another gift is hidden (I helped in the pre-reading years), and runs to retrieve the hidden gift.

Two years ago, the kids even insisted on setting up the train on Mother's Day and Father's Day, hiding our presents and making us search them out in accordance with directions found on the train.

That old line about "the gift that keeps on giving" could surely be applied to the train. Or, if you'll pardon the pun, you could say it was one gift that really delivers!

Anonymous

The Gift That Keeps On Giving

About six years ago, a friend from my husband's job gave him a really goofy gift, a rock with a face painted on it, but a face with a truly silly expression on it. I had seen rocks with faces painted on them before, and I think this was supposed to be a parody on those. It was a real hoot!

But what to do with it? We didn't really need a paperweight, and I don't much go for knickknacks. Since the office friend who gave it to my husband occasionally comes over to the house, I didn't feel comfortable disposing of it, and so I rather uncomfortably set it on top of the bookcase.

When my sister-in-law came to visit, she took one look and said, "What the hell is *that!?*"

Laughing, I explained.

"Boy, I'm glad that guy doesn't work in my husband's office!" my sister-in-law said.

For a gag gift, I wrapped the rock up the following year on my sister-in-law's birthday and gave it to her—along with a few small but "good" presents, of course. She gave it back to me for my birthday, but I returned it the following year.

We've kept it going back and forth every birthday since then. Two years ago my mother got into the act. She made such a joke out of my sister-in-law being "stuck" with the rock, that I gave it to her for Christmas! She returned it for our anniversary, in plenty of time for me to send it to my sister-in-law on her birthday.

Anonymous

New Year's Family Party

We have a family party every New Year's Eve. My wife and I stay home with the kids, and we roast marshmallows in the fireplace, pop corn, drink cocoa, and watch home movies of the kids from years past. They love seeing themselves on film and tape. (We have some of both, as we only recently got a camcorder but had a movie camera in the family for a long time.) We watch Dick Clark on TV and see the New Year come in. Then the kids are packed off to bed.

We hope that they will see New Year's Eve can be a time for family celebrations and doesn't have to be an occasion for drunken carousing. We are trying to set a good example that we hope they will follow in years to come.

We also do a New Year's Resolution kind of thing. We each (parents and kids alike) make a list of Ten Ways I Can Be a Better Person This Year. My wife saves all the lists. Then, on the first of each month, we go over everyone's lists—my wife's and mine too!—and discuss how well each of us is doing at holding to the items on our lists.

Anonymous

Birthday in Bed

Ever since my wife voiced the opinion that breakfast in bed is the height of luxury, our two kids have insisted she have breakfast and dinner in bed on every birthday. They get up and make her breakfast on her birthday, while she sleeps late (or waits patiently in bed reading if she awakens before they're ready).

Breakfast is served on a tray with a flower on it, the flower coming from our garden—though one year it was a dandelion, the kids not yet having learned that the cheery yellow "flower" was actually a weed. In subsequent years, the flowers were more appropriate blooms. (Fortunately, my wife has a spring birthday.)

Dinner is prepared by the kids . . . with a hand from me when needed. It, too, is served in bed, on a tray, with another flower. To tell the truth, my wife associates dinner in bed with illness, not luxury, but she's never hinted at this to the kids. They take too much pleasure in pampering her on her special day.

Anonymous

Birthday Poems

I had two aunts who were very creative, very talented with words. They wrote stories and poems, none of which were ever published, to my knowledge, but many of which delighted family members.

Many years on my birthday, my Aunt Hannah (she liked to be called "Aunt Hank") would write me a poem especially for my birthday. And I remember, one year, a Chanukah poem involving Rudolph the Red-Nosed Reindeer—possibly the only time he made an appearance on Chanukah!

These birthday poems delighted me—what kid wouldn't love a poem written especially for her, with her name worked into it, very clever and creative and funny, too?

Aunt Esther died many years ago. Aunt Hank (she now goes by "Hannah" again) is still alive as I write this, in her late 90s, but retired from poetry-writing as far as I know. I inherited the family writing gene, but I never wrote birthday poems for my daughter and have no nieces or nephews. Perhaps I'll try my hand at birthday poems for my grandson and granddaughter when they get old enough.

C.M.

Thankful Circle

Our family's Thanksgiving tradition is this: Just before sitting down to dinner, we stand in a circle in the living room, holding hands. One by one we each say out loud what we are most thankful for at this time in our lives.

This tradition is one that I intend to carry on when I have children. It can be a good reminder of the things and people that tend to get taken for granted in our daily lives.

Julie Goodwin
Portland, Oregon

Birthday Tape

When our daughter has a birthday, we start recording on the little cassette recorder first thing in the morning. As we wish her happy birthday, the cassette records our wishes for posterity. Then Sheila says a few things into the mike—she's a ham and doesn't need much prompting—about her birthday, what her celebration plans are, how it feels to be a year older than at the time of her last birthday recording, what she hopes the day will bring, and what she hopes the year ahead will bring as well.

Next she opens her presents with the recorder running. With no prompting—she knows the routine by now—she describes her presents for the tape recording. Later, at the party, each of the guests identifies herself and says a few words into the mike.

In the evening, we play back tapes of birthdays past. The average tape probably takes about half an hour. So we can't listen to all the tapes in any one evening, but we always listen to the previous year's and also whichever other ones Sheila decides she wants to hear.

Sometimes, during the year, if Sheila's in a low mood, she'll get out one or more birthday tapes to listen to, and that seems to cheer her up.

Anonymous

S-t-r-e-t-c-h-i-n-g Out Birthdays

We always measured out the birthday presents for our children through the day. There was one present for breakfast, another one for right after school. If we had a small one to give them, we'd throw it in with their lunch.

They enjoyed this; it made their birthdays seem to last longer that way, rather than one big splash and that was it. The children even commented that stretching out the gift-giving made their birthdays seem to go on much longer.

Jerry S. Kosowski
Little Rock, Arkansas

Choice of Menu; Seasonal Goodies

There was a little thing my mother did for all of us when I was growing up in the '50s and early '60s. On anybody's birthday, the birthday person—whether a child or parent—got to choose the entire birthday menu including the dessert. If a child wanted hamburgers and hot dogs on his birthday, that would be the night's meal, even if the night in question was Sunday.

My mother was also an excellent baker, and our house was divided among chocolate lovers and vanilla lovers. But on someone's birthday, they got to choose the dessert.

By the way, my mother always baked appropriately for the seasons, too. On Washington's birthday she always did something with cherries—cherry pie, or cherry tarts—and naturally she baked pumpkin pies for Halloween. There was sheet cake with red, white, and blue icing for the Fourth of July . . . always appropriate to the holiday.

George Hines
Vandergrift, Pennsylvania

Birthday Breakfast

Every birthday is made extra special for our family by letting my kids pick whatever—whatever—they want to eat for breakfast. My oldest boy usually picks a nice logical breakfast. My youngest, however, usually picks candy and ends up with a stomachache for his party. They all enjoy it, however, and look forward to their special birthday breakfast every year.

Cissy Jones

Birthday Seafood

⚒

My mother always offered to cook my brother's or my favorite meal on our respective birthdays. My brother's favorite was beef and broccoli, and that's what we had every year on his birthday. I chose lobster, crab, shrimp . . . basically the whole gamut of seafood possible—the more expensive things, the tastier to the palate. And so, every year on my birthday, we have a big family gathering and cook up large amounts of seafood.

This year, however, I was away at college on my birthday, so my brother wound up with the lobster dinner on his birthday, and for my birthday I ate macaroni and cheese!

Joe Graziano
Goleta, California

July Fourth/Birthday Pig Roast

⚒

July Fourth happens to be my mother-in-law's birthday. We celebrate by all going out to her house in the country and having a pig roast. They get set up for it the night before, roasting the pig, basting it with a butter sauce, and cooking it all night long.

The family makes it a big get-together that lasts the whole weekend. The whole family is invited—we get anywhere from five to thirty people, depending on what else is going on in everyone's lives that weekend.

Patricia Gray
Montz, Louisiana

Family Customs and Traditions

Family Office Celebration

===‖+‖===

We have a family business, so when it's the birthday of someone in the family who works in the office, we have a candle burning in a muffin, or something similar, as a token birthday cake for the celebrant.

In our family it's always been a tradition to go out to dinner to celebrate someone's birthday. The celebrant is the guest of honor in a restaurant, where she or he is given gifts.

Warren Tabachnik
Scarsdale, New York

Every Anniversary Is Special

===‖+‖===

When my parents celebrated their twenty-first anniversary, my brothers and sister and I started planning ahead for the twenty-fifth, thinking we'd like to do something special for a momentous occasion.

"Why wait till then?" one brother asked. "Isn't every anniversary special?" Considering the number of couples who don't make it to anniversary number twenty-five, due to either divorce or death, that seemed eminently sensible, but even assuming my parents would reach their fiftieth anniversary alive, together, and happy, we still had no reason not to treat every anniversary as special.

Well, of course we can't chip in for a fabulous vacation or other expensive once-in-a-lifetime present every year, but there isn't any reason the occasion can't be marked by something more than an ordinary card or flowers or a phone call, or a present that's OK but not really meaningful. So we put our heads together.

For their twenty-second anniversary, our folks got a video-tape of all four of their kids telling them what wonderful parents they had been and why. For their twenty-third anniversary, they got a scrapbook filled with photocopies of mementos and awards that we all have in our individual scrapbooks or keepsake boxes, plus some pictures they didn't have copies of. For their twenty-fourth, we wrote a family history, from our great-great-grandparents down through ourselves, made it into a mini-book (using my sister's computer at work, after hours), and bound it in cloth-covered tagboard and presented it to our parents.

For their twenty-fifth, we indeed sent them on a vacation, as we'd talked about doing years earlier, but you can bet we're not going to neglect their twenty-sixth, or twenty-seventh. . . . We're already putting our heads together to see what kind of plan we can hatch for a special gift to celebrate the next special anniversary, because every anniversary is special: it's the anniversary of our parents.

Anonymous

Birthday Letter

━┽┼┾━

I'm not against enriching Hallmark—it's just that there's no way
a card company can know what I really want to say to someone.
Cards are OK for acquaintances, distant relatives, business
friends, and the like, but for birthdays of close family and close
friends, only a letter will do.

I put a lot of thought into my birthday letters. Sometimes I
write about why I'm proud of the person I'm writing to, what
they've accomplished in the year past, or in their life, or their
finer qualities of which they should be proud; other times it's
what I wish for them in the year ahead.

One year, when one of our daughters was feeling sorry for
herself (somewhat deservedly), I commiserated with her in the
letter, then pointed to all the small but meaningful good things
that had happened in the year past. I didn't take away from or
minimize the year's disappointments and failures, just pointed
out the positive things about the year, too.

Not every year finds me writing the same thing, or even taking the same tack. And every year I manage to say something
different without engaging in bull or in meaningless drivel. If
you think with your heart, you can always find something sin-
cere and worthwhile to say.

Anonymous

Pool Parties

≈┼╪≈

When I was a child, living in South Florida, I was the only one of my friends with a pool in the backyard. My birthday parties were invariably held in our pool; swim trunks were the appropriate dress for my parties, and the entertainment, instead of Pin the Tail on the Donkey, consisted of water polo, keep-away, and other games involving water and perhaps a beach ball. We had swimming races, contests to see who could stay underwater the longest, and all kinds of other wet fun.

Now I have kids, and my kids have a pool in the backyard (still in South Florida), as I did when I was a kid. They have no monopoly on backyard pools; many of their friends have one too. But pool parties seem to have become a family tradition, and instead of pizza parties, bowling parties, or parties with expensive entertainment, our kids invariably ask for a pool party.

And my wife and I have a sort of pool party on our birthdays, as well. We barbecue in the back yard, all of us eating our dinner out there, and we play around in the pool before and after. My wife's birthday is in October, still plenty warm enough for swimming in South Florida, and mine is in March, also usually swimming weather down here. We play games in the water with the kids, and generally have a silly good time.

Anonymous

Family Customs and Traditions

Color-Coded Egg-Hunt

My hairdresser, Keith McHugh, who comes from a large family, has two children of his own. For the past eleven years he's had an Easter egg hunt to which family, friends, and neighbors are invited. He gets fifty or sixty kids at time, all hunting for eggs all over his property.

The eggs he hides are plastic and of different colors. Inside these plastic eggs he puts prizes appropriate to the age of the kids looking for them—he'll have, let's say, the three-to-five-year-olds looking for pink eggs, the six-to-nine-year-olds looking for green eggs, and so forth.

He hides the eggs for the littlest kids in easy places to find, the eggs for somewhat older kids in somewhat harder places, and the hiding places get progressively harder to find with each age group. It goes up to age sixteen; for a sixteen-year-old niece he hid an egg in a tree. (She found the egg and won a certificate to McDonald's.)

He hides as many as two hundred eggs, all outdoors. The kids turn them in after finding them, he puts them all away for a year, then does it again the following Easter. At one point he tried to call off the annual hunt because it was just getting to be too much, but the kids love it and wouldn't let him stop.

Judith Zapadka
Oregon, Ohio

A Geranium for Mother's Day

Although our family didn't have any special traditions for birthdays or anniversaries, there were some things that were traditional in our life.

My parents were very poor, and we kids couldn't afford to buy our mother gifts for Mother's Day. But our father would give us each a few coins, and we'd go to a fruit store that had geraniums. A few coins was enough to buy a geranium—I don't think it was more than a quarter for a plant in those years.

Each one of us, from the oldest to the youngest, would put his or her geranium by the door; then we'd ring the doorbell and run.

My mother was thrilled with the three plants every year.

Gert Ackerman
Boynton Beach, Florida

Bachelor Party Family "Roast"

Our family has a tradition regarding weddings, or more specifically, bachelor parties. In our family, the men of the family have the party together, and only the family attends. No best man, no good buddies, just the family. I myself have four brothers, and our father is one of five brothers, all of whom, along with all of their adult male children, are invited to the parties.

Altogether, over the years, I've been to fifteen of these parties (counting my own bachelor bash), and I've enjoyed every one enormously. There is a fair amount of drinking but no carrying-on with women, no hired belly dancers, nothing for the groom-to-be to have any guilties over when his new wife asks about the party.

One further part of the tradition involves a bit of poking fun at the new groom. Several of the brothers or cousins or uncles or the father get up and "roast" the guest of honor with jokes at his expense. None of us is another Don Rickles, but we've aimed some telling barbs.

Other entertainment of a joking nature also goes on. One year it was a facetious "Last Will & Testament" of what each of us left to the honoree. Many of the jokes were sexual in nature; the rest mostly had to do with marriage in some way. Another year, along the same theme, someone wrote the groom's "Last Will & Testament" of what he was ostensibly leaving to each of us, now that his freedom was dying. Of course it's all good-natured.

Now the oldest boy of the next generation has turned fourteen. There is only one cousin left to be married in our generation, but in another ten or fewer years, we'll probably begin hosting and toasting and roasting the next generation of grooms-to-be.

Anonymous

Memorial Day Remembrance

My wife's uncle (her father's brother) was killed in World War I. In the early 1930s, when she was a girl, this was still a very sensitive matter for her father, and the children never asked questions about their late uncle.

However, once a year, I believe on Memorial Day, her father took the children to a boulevard in Brooklyn—Eastern Parkway?—along which trees had been planted in memory of fallen Brooklyn soldiers. One plaque carried his brother's name, and he always took them to that tree and reminisced at length about the brother he missed so badly.

Anonymous

"Square Easter Eggs"

My mother was—and still is—something of a fanatic on nutrition. She didn't believe in exposing my brother and me to excessive sweets. Halloween and Easter were her two worst nightmares, with all the candy that goes with those two holidays.

There was a limit to what she could do about Halloween; she wasn't about to forbid us to go out trick-or-treating altogether. She did, however, make us turn over our bags of goodies, untouched, for the contents to be rationed out over a period of time. Nobody in our household gorged themselves on Halloween night on Snickers or Hershey's kisses or candy corn; we were honor-bound to bring our bags home intact, and Mom doled the contents out carefully thereafter.

She even carried her beliefs over into her approach to giving out goodies to other people's trick-or-treating children. She bought inexpensive gifts at the five-and-dime and gave them out to visiting trick-or-treaters in lieu of candy.

But it was her approach to Easter that really stands out in my mind. The Easter bunny knew better than to bring baskets of candy to our house. While our friends got huge chocolate bunnies, cream-filled marshmallows, or baskets of assorted little sweets, my brother and I got tiny toy trucks, rubber balls, or boxes of crayons or colored chalk or the like.

We wondered why the bunny singled out our household for the unusual arrangement, when all the other kids got gobs of chocolate and other sweets. "The Easter Bunny respects my wishes. I wrote to him," was my mother's explanation. (When, one year, I skeptically asked Mom what the Easter Bunny's address was, she told me, "The South Pole, of course!")

So on Easter morning, when other kids got baskets that catered to their sweet teeth, my brother and I got little presents, wrapped in floral wrapping paper. (My brother once objected to the flowers on the gift wrap, saying, "That's girl paper," but Mom said, "Flowers are for spring, and Easter is a spring holiday. The Easter Bunny knows.")

My dad was the one who coined the term, "Square eggs" to describe the little boxes—actually, usually oblong rather than square—in which "the Easter Bunny" wrapped our little Easter gifts. "The Easter Bunny brings square eggs to this family," he said jokingly one year, and the term stuck.

The square eggs contained no big gifts, such as at Christmas, no bikes, no expensive toys. But we always received two or three little boxes with something fun in them for each of us, and even after we stopped believing in the Easter Bunny, the tradition of getting "square eggs" for Easter continued, although by then my parents admitted to being the givers.

I'm now a married man with a four-year-old son. Alhough my wife and I let my son eat a pretty fair amount of sweets last Halloween, when he trick-or-treated for the first time, we've already seen to it that the Easter Bunny left some "square eggs" on Easter, with only one small chocolate rabbit. As I child, I resented not getting the goodies that my friends did, but as an adult I can see the wisdom of Mom's decisions.

Let's hear it for "square Easter eggs"—they don't promote cavities or make kids hyperactive. But when my son asks me, some day, where I wrote to the Easter Bunny to request "square eggs" for him instead of so much candy, I don't plan to tell him "The South Pole." When my mother gave me that answer, years ago, it sounded too hokey (although I didn't yet know the word "hokey"), even to my sevenish-year-old ears. Rather, I'll tell my son, "Easter Island."

Anonymous

Turkey and Rabbits, Father and Sons

≈⊣ ⊢≈

One of the fondest memories of my childhood is the way my family celebrated Thanksgiving Day every year.

My father was a hard-working man who spent most of his time making a living for our family. Consequently, he did not have a lot of extra time to spend with my brother and me. When he did have time to spend with us, it was special.

That's why we always looked forward to Thanksgiving Day. We knew we would get to spend the whole day with Dad, and we knew exactly what the day would bring. It was the same every year, and we could hardly wait.

On Thanksgiving morning we would get up early, have a hearty breakfast, put on heavy clothing, and prepare to go rabbit-hunting. Dad would take us to a "secret spot" he knew, and we would spend the entire morning hunting cottontail rabbits and enjoying the special camaraderie that boys have with a father.

Meanwhile, Mom would be busily preparing a Thanksgiving feast for us men in her life. Mom was always an excellent cook, but it seemed that her culinary talents were at their best on Thanksgiving Day.

Early in the afternoon we'd arrive home from our hunting adventure cold and exhausted. The warm house and the delicious smells emanating from the kitchen made us realize how hungry the outdoors and the exertion had made us. We could hardly wait for dinner.

Finally we all sat down to a table covered with enough food to put a serious strain on the table's legs. Then Dad would pray. He thanked the Lord for the food and all the blessings we had received, and he asked for guidance to know how to raise and provide for his family.

Everyone feasted until it seemed that our seams would burst. Finally, after a second piece of pie or cake, we'd retire to the living room, where we'd sit and talk about all the things we were thankful for as we basked in the feeling of warmth and abundance.

Later, after we had all somewhat recovered from overeating, the whole family would gather around the dining room table and play a game until it was time to go to bed.

I never knew if Dad and Mom looked forward to this annual ritual as much as did my brother and I. Dad has gone on to be with the Lord, and Mom lives hundreds of miles away, but the memories still burn brightly and fill my heart with joy.

As I think about the past, it is a Thanksgiving Day family tradition for which I will always be thankful.

Daniel L. Morris
Billings, Montana

Easter Inedible

Every Easter, for almost as long as I can remember, my mother baked a cake in the shape of a lamb. Now, this wasn't just any lamb cake, it was made of some sort of white cake and covered with white icing, then very liberally covered with shredded coconut, which gave it the appearance of a lamb's coat.

The cake always looked like a million dollars, but it tasted like a buck ninety-eight. It was invariably dry as the Sahara, and the coconut was of such a consistency that it always seemed to get caught in our throats.

For years, no one would admit that this cake was anything less than a gastronomic delight, until one year Mom herself remarked that the thing was pretty much inedible. But still, every Easter, the lamb cake made its appearance without fail, and we all laughed together as we politely tried to eat the cake, noteworthy only for its consistency, year in and year out.

Thomas Shearer
Cincinnati, Ohio

Viewing Different Cultures

Both my wife and I are half Greek, though neither of us is Greek Orthodox. But when Easter rolls around we like to take our kids to celebrate both the Protestant and the Orthodox Easter.

The Orthodox Easter involves the bit with the candles and the red Easter egg. (All Easter eggs are dyed red in the Eastern Orthodox religion because the color red symbolizes the blood that Jesus shed.) If you're not familiar with the candles, what it is is that you light a candle at the church and try to get it home without the flame blowing out. It's supposed to be good luck if you succeed.

We like for our kids to see how Easter is celebrated in both versions.

Ted Manos
Roselle, Illinois

Celebrations of Many Lands

Because my family traveled through many countries in the course of my being in the military, we acquired holiday customs from the countries we were in. It wasn't just for Christmas that we celebrated in the manner of other countries. [See "Around-the-World Christmas, page 66.]

For many years, late in February we had Robert Burns Night, when we prepared a meal such as haggis (an inverted sheep's stomach stuffed with meat) and other Scottish foods. We'd drink Scotch whiskey and read some of Burns's poetry.

St. David's Day, another we've celebrated, is a Welsh holiday, involving decorations: daffodils for the lady of the house and a leek for the man of the house are used to decorate the house. We celebrate that in March.

Jerry S. Kosowski
Little Rock, Arkansas

Ugly Eggs and Bunny Money

It seems like families with girls tend to develop customs more than families with all boys do. My husband's family can't recall any traditions other than playing basketball on all the holidays with their dad, while their mom made sandwiches. My family, on the other hand, is steeped in traditions.

One of my favorite holiday traditions concerns Easter. When we'd color eggs, we'd work really hard to make the ugliest egg as well as the prettiest egg. The first person to come to the house after the coloring would be the judge—grandmas, the postman, the drycleaner, someone walking their dog past the house. . . . They'd have to pick the prettiest and the ugliest eggs.

My dad then would tape $1 each onto the prettiest egg and the ugliest egg. He'd leave the eggs out for the Easter Bunny to find and hide, and the Easter Bunny would hide those eggs in the hardest places. The person who found those eggs got to keep the money. (That's the most exciting part, because when you're seven, a dollar's a really big deal!) Most of the time, we'd work real hard to make an ugly egg, and it would turn out to be judged the prettiest egg!

Nobody in the family is the right age to hunt eggs now, but we're moving on to the next generation. They're infants now, too young to hunt eggs, but they will be old enough soon. I plan to keep up the tradition with my own daughter.

Kathleen Parrish
Spokane, Washington

Ceremonial Wine Encore

We're Orthodox Jews and have a small tradition in our family that goes from father to son and has been going on for five generations now. This tradition centers around the bris [circumcision] ceremony, although what we do is not Jewish law but our family's own tradition.

At a bris, a little wine is put on the baby's lips. Our family puts away the unused portion of the bottle of wine, and when the son is married, the wine is given to him at the wedding ceremony. The groom drinks a sip of wine from this bottle that was originally opened at the time of his bris.

Fred Weiser
Cleveland Heights, Ohio

Vodka and Bread

Our family has adapted an old Russian wedding tradition. When someone in the family gets married, the first thing after the wedding, the couple and the wedding attendants head back to the home of the mother of the bride. The entire bridal party takes shots of vodka and breaks bread—literally bread—there. Only after that do they proceed to the larger reception.

Michael Getzie
Lake Worth, Florida

Sharing with Outsiders

A neat custom about holidays in our family is that my mom always used to try to invite somebody outside the family, a custom that we've continued. For instance, this year at Thanksgiving, I invited two Filipino women who are working for one year at a nursing home here. It was very interesting— their culture is so different.

We have also hosted missionaries. I realized the culture difference when I tried to explain baseball-card-collecting to a missionary from India who supports fifteen pastors and churches on $15,000 a year.

Sherry Yeaton
Epsom, New Hampshire

Gathering Bittersweet

My grandmother always had bittersweet on her Thanksgiving table, so my mother's been taking me out to collect bittersweet for the Thanksgiving table since I was very small. (Bittersweet is all that's colorful at Thanksgiving time in Ohio.)

We live in a rural area; in fact there are woods behind my house, and lately that's where we've gone wandering to get the bittersweet.

When my son was younger, I took him out to gather bittersweet, but now that he's older, he doesn't go. It's different between mothers and sons than between mothers and daughters. I look forward to the day I have grandchildren and can take them out to gather bittersweet.

The thing that sticks in my mind about bittersweet is that it only shows its bright colors when it's dried and aging. My mother always told me that it symbolizes that there's beauty in aging.

Robyne Gardner
Port Clinton, Ohio

Strudel . . . from the Heart

One of our family's nicest traditions, which unfortunately has ceased to exist, is one that my mother and aunts brought with them from Europe. When anyone got married, they would make strudel and give it as a gift for the reception.

When they came to America and settled in Louisville, Kentucky, they were all busy, everyone worked, but they always managed to come up with several thousand pieces of strudel for a wedding in the family. That number is not an exaggeration— I literally mean several thousand pieces.

This isn't the normal large strudel with large pieces of apple. This was hand minced. There were no food processors then, no quick way out. This wasn't a project that could be undertaken sitting down, either. You had to stand to hand-chop nuts, hand-mince citrus and raisins and cherries. It was truly a labor of love.

It was an enormous gift. I can remember the bowl that the filling had to go into. It was approximately twenty-nine or thirty inches wide, and fit across the entire width of our refrigerator. It was probably at least ten inches tall—a huge container—and there were two of them.

All of that filling went into strudel, a pulled dough. One would roll and stretch it by hand. The finished strudel was the size of a fifty-cent piece. All the pieces looked alike, as if they'd come off a machine, but it was all done by hand, and carefully. They didn't want any pieces not to match; they wanted it to look just right. Each piece was dusted with cinnamon and glazed with oil prior to baking, and decorated with love. That's what went into the strudel—love.

My family included nineteen cousins. For them the strudel symbolized many things—the extreme care taken on behalf of all of us to insure that we always had family *simchas* [joy] together. Also for me, personally, it symbolized that these women were willing to go to great lengths for the benefit of each one of us. The aunts and my mother were extremely tired from all they had to do, yet they managed to get together enough strength for this tremendous undertaking.

This tradition stopped in the last three years, since my mother and the last of my aunts passed away. With their passing, it's something that we, as cousins, can do individually, even though we're a more scattered family, not all living in the same community any more.

But even though we all could do it, it wouldn't be the same. Even our best efforts would never match up to theirs.

Renee Solomon
Toledo, Ohio

Grandmother's China

My very favorite tradition in the family is a very old one. My grandmother has a spectacular collection of bone china. Each place setting has a different pattern; no two are the same. All the holiday tables are set this way, and the effect is stunning. The colors and the patterns are so beautiful. When each of the females in the family (my sisters, cousins, aunts, mother, etc.) reaches a certain age, my grandmother gives her one of her place settings with which to start a collection.

After that, for all major events (weddings, births, Christmas), she gives her another place setting of her china. It is her goal that by the time she is gone, all of us will have our own collections started with all of her china. Our memories of her will live forever every time we look into our dining rooms or set a formal table!

Kathleen Parrish
Spokane, Washington

Of Family, Books, and Togetherness

※+↔※

In the family I grew up in, we celebrated special occasions by gathering for good talk, good laughs, and maybe a special meal—maybe a home-cooked one, or a picnic, or we walked on foot to the drugstore for delicious toasted sandwiches and "lime dopes"—as Cokes used to be called in Alabama.

I still recall with delight the fun and excitement of getting together with dear relatives from far-off places to exchange news and funny happenings, both new ones and those remembered from long ago.

Books were important to many family members; they were often carefully selected and given for presents. This is still true for us today—books are still important. And I love certain magazine articles, Mike Royko and other syndicated columnists, and the newsletter *The Prairie Rambler.*

Today, when our daughters and their families and in-laws come from other states for a small reunion (sometimes only a few people, sometimes thirteen or so), the rafters ring with the sound of happy voices and laughter.

Like so many families I know, we are happiest when we get together. Food is simple, but there is plenty to snack on and lots of soft drinks. The daughters bring special dessert treats and other non-perishable foods. I appreciate this, as I'm not much of a cook, but I do get something on the table three times a day.

I could go on and on, but I'm thinking of my new P.G. Wodehouse, and I've just got to go read another chapter in it!

Mary Curtis
Pensacola, Florida

Breakfast Parties

My mother used to give breakfast parties the way other people give dinner parties. She'd invite both her friends and the family, and there'd be too many people to all sit down to eat at once. One segment of the family would come one hour, another part of the family the next, and the third shift would be her friends. The parties were held outdoors, in my parents' back yard, and my mother made all the food herself, including traditional Jewish dishes like pickled herring and pickles.

My father would lug heavy, solid wood picnic tables from the basement to the backyard. There was a hammock, a little kids' wading pool, and card tables, at which the guests played card games. The food was wonderful!

Linda Becker
West Palm Beach, Florida

Decoration Day Family Get-Together

⇌+⇌

Every year, usually over Memorial Day weekend or around then, my family gets together for a couple of days in the rural area in far western Kentucky where my mom was born. It's a family reunion, combined with the local Memorial Day celebration.

Around there, the holiday is called Decoration Day, and involves decorating graves with flowers and little flags. We also take pictures of our living family members next to headstones of family members who've died. At the cemetery I show my kids the graves of their ancestors and other family members. "This was your great-aunt," or whoever.

In that part of the country, a lot of the families are related. We all meet at a little church, where there's a memorial service; everybody gets together for a huge pot-luck thing—perhaps fifty or sixty people. We eat a lot, visit, and have a good time. The people who still live in the area cook food for the pot luck, and some of us who aren't local to the area might bring barbecue from a good barbecue place.

My kids get to see the part of the country their great-great-I-don't-know-how-many-greats-grandparents settled. My mom's family came there originally on land grants given to the people who fought in the Revolutionary War. The visit gives my kids (now five and six) a sense of our relationship to the country.

Ted Manos
Roselle, Illinois

Invented Holidays

So many reasons may be found to celebrate; so many opportunities exist for family happenings or special events. Not all these reasons can be found in days specially marked on the calendar, but why let that stop you from making a special occasion out of what appears to be an ordinary day? Calendar-makers have never heard of Arrival Day, Back-to-School Holiday, New Season, or Midsummer Holiday, but that doesn't stop certain families from celebrating them.

"Steal" one of these holidays for your own enjoyment . . . or invent one on your own. Can you, your spouse, or one of your parents claim to be a "new American"? Celebrate as Citizenship Day the day you (or your parent) took your (his/her) oath as an American, and instill patriotic pride in your child. Or find some other reason—or good excuse—to celebrate a holiday that's unique to your family.

Arrival Day

＝＋＋＝

Every year in late January, our family celebrates Arrival Day, a made-up holiday in honor of our ancestors' arrival in America. We don't actually know when our various ancestors got here, and certainly with all the great-grandparents and great-great-grandparents involved in the emigration, we couldn't celebrate once for each arriving ancestor. So I arbitrarily picked late January.

It's a time when everyone's in the winter doldrums, and there haven't been any major holidays since the Christmas season ended. It seems like a time when we could all stand the lift a holiday brings us.

My husband and I cook ethnic dishes for dinner on Arrival Day, choosing from among recipes from one or more of the many countries we can trace ancestors back to. (We like to say our kids have more different kinds of ethnicity in them than Domino's has kinds of pizza toppings!)

We used to go all-out with decorations suggestive of one or more of the countries to which we can trace back our ancestry, and one year we even did ethnic costumes, but the kids seem to have outgrown that aspect of the celebration, averring that it was "dorky," so now we leave out the decorations and costumes. They're still comfortable with the rest of what we do to celebrate.

It's a night for recounting the various "coming-over" stories of different family members in the past. It's a night for telling old family stories, discussing what America was like at the time our various ancestors immigrated here, discussing ethnic traditions from some of the "old countries," and singing patriotic songs. It's a night when we all discuss what it means to be an American, and why we should consider ourselves lucky to live here.

Anonymous

Celebrating Learning

Our family has always prized education, so when I heard my kids groaning over the start of a new school year, I knew I wanted to do something about it to enforce a more positive attitude in them. Not that I think the Back to School Holiday we instituted has created a 180° turnaround in their attitudes, but it has helped.

The day before the first day of school is a holiday at our house. The kids get to sleep late—for the last time on a weekday. They're also exempt from making their beds—the one day a year they're permitted to skip that chore. After a big brunch featuring their favorite foods, we make a trip to the book store, where each child gets to select two books.

Next comes a trip to get any last-minute school supplies I haven't already bought. There's always something. Then we purchase something educational for the family. It could be a disk for the CD-ROM, an educational videotape, a new globe . . . but it's always something that benefits the whole family.

Often during the year we'll quiz the kids over dinner, asking them questions about subjects they're learning in school, or just things we feel they ought to know. But at dinner on Back to School Holiday night, they're the quizmasters and get to ask the two of us questions, pitting Mom and Dad against each other to see who scores the highest (and jeering mercilessly but not really unkindly whenever we miss a question). Dinner itself is always some kind of special treat.

After dinner we get serious, writing out "contracts" with the kids. Each child has to sign his or her contract, stipulating that s/he's going to start his/her homework within an hour of getting home from school, without having to be bugged about it, and will finish all homework, including any necessary studying for tests, before watching TV, playing videogames, getting involved in any long phone conversations, or anything else recreational. Weekend homework is to be completed by 5 PM on Sunday unless specific permission has been given otherwise.

Various other clauses are added to the contracts from year to year as we feel they are needed, based on situations or problems we've encountered with each child in the year preceding. But the net effect of each contract is to get the child to agree to the necessary study habits in advance, thus heading off any number of hassles during the school year. The kids understand what's required of them, and we don't get too much arguing or fudging.

After that we roast marshmallows in the fireplace, and we usually play one of the knowledge-intensive boxed games we have, like Trivial Pursuit or Jeopardy.

The day ends with early bedtime, so the kids can wake up refreshed for the first day of school.

Anonymous

Family Customs and Traditions

Midsummer's Eve Cards and Letters

I've long regretted that so much time passes from one Christmas to the next. Christmas is a time of good feelings, of getting in touch, and of sending family letters, those little photocopied or computer-copied missives that catch everyone up on news from your family.

So for the last four years I've adopted the custom of buying some of those wildlife cards with the pretty fronts and blank insides, and sending them out to everyone on my Christmas list as Midsummer's Eve cards.

"HAPPY MIDSUMMER'S EVE," I always write (or type) in them. "JUST A CARD AND LETTER TO KEEP IN TOUCH AND LET YOU KNOW YOU'RE THOUGHT OF THROUGH THE YEAR. HOPE YOU'RE HAVING A WONDERFUL SUMMER. JOY TO ALL." Then I sign all our names (myself, my husband, and our two kids) and enclose the "family letter—midsummer edition," in which I catch everyone up on the doings of our family since the Christmas letter went out.

It's my little attempt to capture just a bit of the special feeling that's in the air at Christmas time, some of which comes from knowing you're remembered by people far and wide. I must have made a positive impression on at least one friend; she's now sending out floral-motif cards to everyone on her Christmas list to celebrate the first day of spring!

Anonymous

Aunt's Day

My mom's two sisters live nearby, and because they're a real close-knit family, our aunts had a lot to do with raising us. My sister and I decided early on that it was a shame there was no "Aunts' Day" like there is a Mothers' Day and a Fathers' Day, so we invented one.

We declared the third Sunday in April "Aunts' Day" and asked Mom to invite our two aunts over to celebrate. My sister and I made cards, since there was nothing available commercially, and we bought presents. We also helped Mom cook the dinner, and we made it extra-special. We gave them presents at dinner, and made a big fuss over the two of them. They were most appreciative.

We've celebrated "Aunts' Day" in our family ever since—always the third Sunday in April. We don't celebrate the same way every year, but we always give a homemade card and a present, and we always make some kind of a fuss over them. My aunts appreciate it a lot.

Anonymous

Half-Holidays

※+┼≈

My mother must have felt there weren't enough holidays in the calendar; she celebrated half-birthdays, Christmas-in-July, and New Season (four times a year).

Half-birthdays were celebrated pretty much like regular birthdays, except the party was just for family. Each celebrant got a present, a special dinner in his or her honor (at which s/he got to choose the menu), and the privilege of staying up past his or her bedtime.

Christmas-in-July involved an exchange of presents, a pine branch decorated with a few red balls and saved-over tinsel, and a huge feast complete with roast ham.

New Season came four times a year, of course. In the spring we celebrated the rebirth that spring is, the return of livable temperatures, the new growth all around us outdoors, and the baby birds we knew we'd soon have in our trees. Dinner was prepared by us kids, with as much supervision and help as we required.

In the summer we celebrated with a picnic. We played tag and other outdoor games. (When I say "we" I mean all of us; Mom and Dad joined in.)

Fall's celebration was a harvest festival. I recognize that the harvest was the reason behind Thanksgiving originally, but the harvest aspect of the November holiday has gotten away from most of us in recent times. Our fall celebration included the harvest aspect.

We also were supposed to celebrate back-to-school, an angle of the holiday that didn't meet with the approval of my older sister or myself. Only my younger sister—who *liked* school, to the amazement and disgust of my older sister and me—really threw herself into that aspect of the celebration.

New Season for winter was a quiet celebration, as befits a season of dormancy. Besides, Christmas was right around the corner. But it was still an occasion to celebrate, to be happy, and to reflect on the gifts the earth gives us. (In winter, nature's least giving season, we concentrated on snow to play in and clean air to breathe.) We had a fireplace, and our New Season winter celebration always included roasting marshmallows in the fireplace. (My dad did the roasting; we kids handled the "chore" of eating.)

Mom always decorated the dining room table in accordance with the season. For spring she'd always find one bud on a stem to put in water on the table; summer offered bountiful flowers (including, sometimes, a dandelion or two!); for fall she'd find a few brown leaves, though the trees weren't really turning yet; in winter, it was pine boughs and pine cones.

We exchanged presents, and each of us had to stand up and make a statement—however brief—about what the season meant to us. The presents weren't extravagant; we each got one small gift, but it was always something good. Perhaps a small, inexpensive paint set, or a stack of new comic books, or a book, or some other little but much-appreciated toy.

My mother was—still is—a very happy, very "up" person, and I think she was glad of any excuse for a celebration, but I think she also knew that all these made-up occasions had a real benefit to them as well. They drew us together, reinforced our sense of family, and gave us something we felt belonged to "just us."

Anonymous

Midsummer Resolutions

Our family has an unusual tradition that I've never run across anywhere else. It started about twelve years ago.

I was chiding our son for some bad habits and reminded him that one of his New Year's resolutions was to keep his room neat, and another was to improve his table manners. He had made an earnest effort for about a month, but then had slid back into his old ways.

He protested and griped when I got on him about his failing to keep up on his resolutions, and at some point in the conversation he whined, "Aw, Ma! That was way back in January!"

I started to snap back, "Does that give you the right to break all your resolutions?" but then I thought better of it. A year is a long time, especially for a child that young. (And, really, for all of us—how many of us adults keep all our resolutions? How many of us even keep most of them for even half a year?)

And thus was born our Midsummer Resolutions.

One night sometime in July—not necessarily the same date every year—we build a fire in the fireplace (despite the heat) and all gather around it. We toast marshmallows and talk about our New Year's resolutions, which I've kept a copy of.

Everyone—and that includes us parents—talks about how well he or she has done in keeping up with his/her resolutions. (No comments or criticisms from other family members are permitted.) Each of us then renews his/her resolve to improve himself/herself, repeating the same resolutions we made on New Year's Day. (We are also free to add new resolutions if we want, but this is not required.)

Then I make some hot cocoa and serve it, and we all "toast"

our renewed resolutions with the cold-weather beverage. After that, it's back to summer life as usual—except that we're all conscious of our renewed resolve to improve ourselves, and conscious that our fellow family-members are watching us to see how well we do at sticking to our resolutions.

The little mid-year renewal gives a boost to our resolve, and because we know through the first half of the year that Midsummer Resolution Night is coming is, I suspect, an influence on us to keep us more committed to holding to our New Year's resolutions.

Anonymous

Chasing the Midwinter Doldrums

The only bad part of Christmas is the letdown that follows. For a month (or longer, if you succumb to the merchants' hype) you've been building yourself up for Christmas.

There's the shopping, baking, cooking, wrapping presents, sending off parcels to distant relatives and friends, the round of parties, visits to Santa when the kids are younger, the big morning complete with opening presents, the huge feast on Christmas Day, and enjoying the presents afterward. There's a shelf full of Christmas cards to enjoy, and letters from people you might not have heard from since last Christmas. There's egg nog and pumpkin pie, feeling good in church, and taking part in the pageant.

Even when Christmas itself is over, there's still the tree to look at for a week longer, and excitement in the air as New Year's approaches.

But after New Year's Day—depression! When the bowl

games are over, the last bit of egg nog and leftover dip is gone, the presents have grown old, the last bit of Christmas turkey has been digested, and the festive decorations have all been dismantled, what's left but a great big letdown?

We have a family party on the second weekend in January. Just the four of us. It gives us something to look forward to. We light a fire in the fireplace and, pushing the large rug out of the way, we eat dinner on the floor around the fire.

The kids get to plan the menu . . . and some years the menu is pretty zany. Nutrition rules go out the window just this once. The only requirements are that it be food that can be eaten informally and that it not cost an arm and a leg.

After dinner we exchange homemade presents—nothing that's going to bankrupt anyone's piggybank—and then we have family talent night. We follow that up with games, all the fun games we can think of. And now that the kids are older, we can play even better games. Mad Libs, charades, Botticelli . . . the list varies from year to year, but we always play the kinds of games that provoke laughter.

Because our party is held on a Saturday night, it's an occasion for staying up late, way past the kids' bedtimes, which is yet another treat for them.

Post-Christmas letdown? We've got the cure!

Anonymous

Midsummer Holiday

Around the middle to end of August every year, our kids get restless. My wife's theory is that they're antsy about the approach of school; my own belief is that they've had too much leisure and miss the structure of the school year. Whichever of us is right—and for all I know, we may both be wrong—the bottom line is that we have three restless boys.

It's a time when we haven't celebrated a formal holiday since the Fourth of July, which nobody makes a big deal out of around here anyhow. Fireworks are illegal, the prohibition is strictly enforced, and that's the part of Fourth of July that kids most relate to. So by mid- to late August, the kids are hungry for a holiday.

As a teacher, I have the summer off (while my wife works), so most of the preparations for Midsummer Holiday fall on me and the boys. We prepare a big picnic feast. Some years, we've held the picnic in our own back yard; other times, we've gone to various parks' picnic areas. Besides eating our picnic dinner, we play outdoor games (races and such). What other activities we get into depend on where we are.

If we stay home, we have our big backyard pool for swimming races and generally splashing around. If we go to a park that has campfire facilities, we'll build a fire, cook s'mores for dessert, and tell ghost stories around the campfire. One year we borrowed a big tent from friends, set up the tent in the backyard, and had a backyard camp-out, again with ghost stories—this time in complete darkness. Whatever we do, the boys always stay up way past their bedtime—which is relaxed to begin with, over the summer.

Different years have featured different activities. Some years' activities have been really elaborate, other years' more simple. Any preparations that are involved fall on my shoulders as "summer househusband." One year we made a long weekend of it, camping out at a not-too-distant campground; but we decided we really weren't that much of an outdoorsy family, and we haven't repeated that particular type of celebration.

Some years I think Midsummer Holiday is such a good idea, they ought to make a national holiday out of it. But most of the time, I'm kind of glad we can claim it for our family's very own.

Anonymous

Keeping in Touch

Keeping in touch with family is important, whether it's extended family in distant cities whom you want to exchange news with, or immediate family, temporarily relocated, who need a word from home to make faraway seem less lonely. It may be to your cousins, who are spread out from Ashtabula to Yaphank, or your kids, away at summer camp, with whom you're wanting to keep in close contact. In any case, you need to keep in touch, spread the news, and make sure an "I-Love-You" message is heard or read. And you need to get together with those distant relatives, too.

Here are a few ways that families keep in touch.

Taped Round Robin

※┼┼※

I come from a large family (I have two brothers and two sisters). Of course we all talk on the phone, but between the constraints of time and the fact that there's bound to be at least one child pestering Mommy or Daddy to get off the phone, or interruptions via Call Waiting, it's really difficult for all five of us to be completely caught up on each other's lives.

So we keep a Round Robin tape going around the family.

At first, it was a letter we circulated, rather than a tape. Each brother/sister typed her/his contribution to the family annals, enclosed it with his/her siblings' contributions, and sent it on to the next person on the list. Now we find that a tape takes less time to make (especially for the two siblings who are still computer-less), and we all have the pleasure of actually hearing our siblings' voices.

The sibling who receives the tape listens to his/her four siblings' reports on what's going on in her/his family, then adds his/her own report to the end of the tape. If the tape is near the end, the recipient will contribute a new tape, recording on it, enclosing the old tape (with four reports on it) and the new tape (with his/her report on it) when s/he sends it to the next sibling in the circle. Each sibling, receiving the tape, erases his/her last report, which is now at the beginning (possibly the beginning of the first of two tapes), substituting a new report at the end (possibly the end of the second of two tapes). And so it goes, continually making the cycle, one or two tapes with news (and sometimes opinions, on anything from family matters to politics!) from each sibling in turn.

We all still talk on the phone to each other, every week or

two, but now we get most of our news from the tapes, which each sibling is honor bound not to keep in his/her house more than three days before recording his/her contribution and sending it on.

Anonymous

"Cousins' Courier"

My two sisters and my husband's sister and brother all live near enough to get together for special occasions but not near enough to see each other often. Because our house is centrally located to the various other families, and because it's fairly large, it's usually the focal point of the family gatherings. Christmas, Thanksgiving, Mothers' Day, Fathers' Day, Fourth of July, Memorial Day, Labor Day, and sometimes other weekends as well will often find most or all of our respective siblings, their spouses, and their offspring at our house. Two of the families in question have RVs they can sleep in; the rest either sleep at our house, camping out on the living room floor if need be, or take rooms at a nearby motel.

With such frequent gatherings, you can understand that our respective kids have grown close to each other. They take an interest in the goings-on in their various cousins' lives and used to look to their parents to fill them in on any news.

No longer. Now there's the *Cousins' Courier*. Produced semi-regularly on our computer by my daughter, it contains news of all the kids of her generation, all the cousins on both sides of the family, my husband's side and mine. She calls up and gets the news, honor-bound not to chat overlong with any one family (it's long distance), then produces the paper and runs off a copy for every branch of the family. These she mails out to each branch, giving the kids a chance to catch up on each other's news and ensuring a continuing bonding among all the cousins at the same time.

We adults read it too, so we know what the kids are up to.

Anonymous

Packing Love Notes

My husband travels for a living; he used to travel all over the world. When he was leaving for a trip, I'd put a note in his briefcase wishing him luck and telling him to hurry back. When he got retrained for a new field and started school, I did the same thing, putting a note in that said "Good luck and get home safely."

He always looked for my note when he traveled. If on occasion he didn't find one, he'd get nervous.

Laury Egan
Bethpage, New York

Whole-Family Newsletter

Every year some of the people on my mom's side of the family put together a family newsletter. It's kind of a reunion in print. Normally they want all the information for the newsletter submitted to them by November so they can have it all together in time to get the newsletter out for Christmas. Family members from all around the world send in information about what's going on with their particular branch of the family.

The newsletter is broken down by the last names, and within each last name it's broken down by geographic area—for example, the Burkes of Akron, Ohio, the Burkes of New Mexico, etc. The newsletter tells what's new within each branch of the family, and what they're doing. My own personal first entry will be this year.

The first year, the newsletter was four pages long, and it's growing. It keeps everyone in the family posted on what's happening with everyone else.

An address and phone number is listed for everyone who's in the newsletter, so any other relative who reads about someone and says, "Oh, I see so-and-so is doing this-and-such; I think I'll call him," can get in touch.

Tom Cardarelli
Akron, Ohio

Family Customs and Traditions

Family Get-Togethers

〰✦✦〰

I have four sisters and two brothers. Our entire family likes to get together, but after we all got older, got married, and had children of our own, there were a lot of us, and my mother said, "Enough is enough—the house isn't big enough for everybody!" But we still liked the idea of getting together—sometimes at holidays, sometimes in the fall, when there are several family birthdays, or sometimes just whenever. One of us, however, has to bite the bullet and take on hosting the whole group.

Usually it runs to thirty-five to forty people of various ages and sizes. The person who's hosting the get-together is responsible for making the meat and potatoes for the meal, and everyone else brings the side dishes, although sometimes they bring main courses too.

For instance, for Easter I said I'd be the hostess. I made a ham, mashed potatoes, and gravy. Other people brought lamb, kielbasa, beef loin . . . we had five entrees altogether. And everyone else brought vegetables, salad, and other things. You never know what you're going to get—dessert, hors d'oeuvres, wine. . . . It was a very nice gathering.

I'd just assumed everybody did this, but most of my friends' families don't.

Judith Zapadka
Oregon, Ohio

Extending the Season

≈‖≈

This tradition started quite by accident, when my husband had just gotten into the real estate business.

In real estate you have a lot of clients and other people you want to keep in touch with. At Christmastime, my husband wanted to send cards to all these people, but we're not normally Christmas-card senders, and we ended up sending the cards really late. It was after January 1 when we finally got them out in the mail. So we put a letter in the card, as other people do, going through the highlights of our year.

We expected a lot of criticism because the cards were so late, but the reaction we got was totally the opposite; the people loved them. It brought back the last little spark of the holiday season for them, after they'd put the season away for another year.

Now we do it every year, enclosing a letter with the card and sending the cards out late. We always make our letter very humorous, and people enjoy reading it. We enjoy doing it, too, because it gives us a chance to look back on the year, reflect on what we've accomplished, and that sort of thing. People enjoy the late cards so much more—it means so much more to them, because it gives them the last little look at the holiday season.

Trish Overgard
Midlothian, Virginia

Family Is Family

꞊꜀ ꜀꞊

"Family is family," my mom always used to say. She meant that family is important, family sticks by each other, family can be counted on, and even if one of them does something not-nice to you, they're still your family and you should stick by them.

Reinforcing this belief, she had a get-together for the family every month. Whoever lived within driving distance would come, and rare was the occasion when one of them pleaded a prior engagement and missed out on the occasion.

Our house was always the scene of the get-together. For some reason (and I don't know if it was Mom's choice or what), none of the other relatives ever hosted the get-together. But Mom didn't make herself crazy (or broke) cooking a huge meal for everyone. Some months it was just snacks on a Sunday afternoon, and everyone went home in time for dinner. Other months it was a full dinner, but it was a covered-dish supper to which everyone brought something to eat.

Family members were encouraged to bring other things besides food. If an out-of-state daughter had sent pictures of her latest child, or a son at college had sent home a photo, if a child had gotten an "A" on a school paper, or a three-year-old had a scribbled drawing he was especially proud of, bringing it along was encouraged.

My brother's enthusiasm for dinosaurs got its start at one of these family get-togethers, and my interest in the work of Mark Twain was a direct result of a cousin's enthusiastic raving over a book by Twain (I forget which one now) that she had just finished.

We got to see dinosaur models and model airplanes, stamp

collections and homemade books. More than one cousin recited a poem, did a magic trick, or sang, showing off a real or imagined talent.

The adults exchanged child-raising hints and recipes, gardening hints and bits of family lore. There was always a lot of storytelling. ("Remember the story of Uncle Louie and the vacuum-cleaner salesman?" "I forget the details. Tell it again." Or "How old was Great-Grandma Ethel when her parents brought her over from the old country?" "I don't remember. I don't even remember where they emigrated from. Randy, do you remember?") We kids picked up a lot of family history and reinforced our sense of belonging.

It's a custom I'd love to perpetuate, but unfortunately we're the only family members living in the Kansas City area.

Anonymous

Family Customs and Traditions

Family Auction

Every two or three years we have a family reunion, which includes a huge dinner. The dinner is funded by an auction, to which everyone brings something family-oriented. Last time, the dinner was a catered outdoors affair, with ten round tables seating ten people each, nice tablecloths, and lots of buffet-style food. It cost around $1600 to feed the one hundred people who attended—and that $1600 is just about what the proceeds from the auction came to.

Everyone is expected to contribute one item for the auction, and everything has to be related to the family in some way, either because it was crafted by a family member or because it's a picture or other representation of a family member. People bring watercolors they've painted, pottery, banners, craftsy sorts of things. . . . Some have baked cookies and made chocolate sauce for the auction. The contribution may be an old trophy or piece of jewelry belonging to a member of the family, a t-shirt representing a team a family member has been on, a bumper sticker from the political campaign of a family member—but there has to be a family connection. We had to tell one of my aunts, "This is not a garage sale, Ruthie!"

Not only does the auction raise money for the dinner, but when the items are auctioned off, you learn so much about what's going on in your family. The story is told as the item is held up to be auctioned off.

Janebell Crowe
Richardson, Texas

Family Love Notes

My father used to travel on business, and my mother would have us write little notes to Dad and hide them in all the articles of clothing that she would pack for him to take with him on his trip. He traveled about every two to three months.

The contents of the notes were simple. "Daddy, I love you." Or, with a homemade picture, "This is a picture of me. I hope you have a good time." And all the other things little kids say. It was the thought that counted.

My mother left notes for us kids, too. She'd put them in my brother's and my socks when she rolled them up, or she stuck them in our pjs and other clothes when we were going off to camp.

Linda Becker
West Palm Beach, Florida

Round Robin Catch-up

Our extended family is quite large—siblings, close cousins, and branches of all these families. We're close-knit but widespread, living in many different states. If each member of the family were to talk to each other member of the family it would be not only prohibitively time-consuming but also injurious to the wallet (in terms of long distance costs). So we instituted a Round Robin phone rotation.

While any family member is of course free to call any other family member and talk at length about anything, certain family members are scheduled to call certain other family members on preset days of the week, relaying whatever news there is about all the family members.

For instance, I call my sister Grace every Tuesday. My sister Mariette has called me on Monday. From her, I get whatever news there is of the family, taking notes as she talks. Then when I call Grace on Tuesday, I relay all the info I've made notes on from my conversation with Mariette. Grace in turn will pass it all along to cousin Bob, who's next on the Round Robin. Since we each get called every week, no one's ever more than a week behind in the news.

And, as I indicated above, anyone is free to call anyone out of rotation at any time. So if Mariette tells me cousin Ellie is having a problem with her son, and it sounds like something I went through with mine, and I think I have some good advice for her, I can always pick up the phone and call her directly.

These weekly catch-up conversations tend to be lengthy, but it would involve far more time on the phone to talk to each family member one at a time every week. The other alternative would be to talk to everyone individually but far less often. For a close-knit group like us, that wouldn't be satisfactory; we like to know the ins and outs of each other's lives more intimately than an occasional phone call would provide. This way we're current on family news and gossip, and we can still talk to any sibling, cousin, niece, nephew, aunt, or uncle directly, any time we want to pick up the phone and make contact.

Anonymous

Traditions Rooted in Superstition

The reasons behind some traditions are pretty obvious, while others are more obscure. But with most traditions that have discernible rationales behind them, the reasons are at least somewhat sensible.

Not so the traditions and customs in this section. They are, admittedly, born of superstition. They've caught on, however, and they've taken a firm hold in these families.

I offer them to you not with the intention of disseminating superstition but for two other reasons—good reasons. One is that it's always interesting to learn of other families' traditions, even when we have no intention of adopting them ourselves. The other is that in reading of a tradition, the account of it may spark something in our minds, leading us to say, "Hey, wouldn't it be a great idea if we _____?" And you're off on a twist of an idea you just read, turning the idea around, turning it into something else, a great idea that perhaps only marginally resembles what you just read about.

Maybe you'll get such an inspiration from something in here. If not, you'll at least enjoy reading these little accounts of superstition-based traditions.

Bragging Rites

This tradition may seem quaint, even weird, in the modern age: Whenever anyone in our family bragged on anything you had (like "That's a nice shirt"), you were expected to offer to give it to them on the spot! The theory behind this was that if anyone had something good enough to brag about, the evil spirits might overhear them bragging, in which case they'd arrange for you to lose it one way or another. Therefore, it was just as well for you to give it up right then and there, rather than wait to lose it.

The same logic, by the way, applied to such a simple thing as answering when someone asked, "How are you doing?" Nowadays, people automatically say, "Fine," but back in Appalachia, where we worried about the evil spirits hearing us, the standard reply was "Tolerable, just tolerable" (pronounced "tol'able," and spoken with as much pain as could be put into the voice).

Herbert D. Tabor
South Houston, Texas

In-and-Out, Never on Friday

There are two traditions that I guess you could call superstitions in my wife's family. They've been handed down through the family.

If my in-laws enter a home through a specific door, they feel they must leave through the same door. If they leave through a different door than the one they entered through, they believe ill fate will meet them. It's hilarious, and we all make light of it, but they're very serious about it.

At one time they came to our house and there was a snow-storm while they were here. The easier way out to their car would have been through the garage, but that was *not* the door they'd entered through, so they were *not* leaving that way. They walked the entire length of our walkway battling snowdrifts to go out the same way they came in.

They're getting older now, and when they leave someone's house they have to stop and reflect on which door they entered through, but they wouldn't dream of leaving by a different door.

They have another quirk too, that has been handed down in the family. They absolutely believe it is bad luck to sign any legal documents or make a purchase of any size on a Friday.

My wife and I are both forty-four and have been married since our early twenties, so we've been living with this one a long time. At one time we purchased a house, and the closing was scheduled for a Friday. My wife's mother, when she heard about it, behaved in such an outlandish way that we had to postpone the closing. She was convinced that bad luck would occur to us if we signed the papers on a Friday!

Al Parinello
Old Tappan, New Jersey

Rice, Loose Change, and Herring

══╬╪══

My grandmother had a peculiar New Year's Eve custom. She'd pour some rice into a napkin and throw some loose change in with it, then tie the napkin up. At the stroke of midnight, she'd throw the package out the apartment window. At the same time, she'd eat pickled herring. I am not making this up!

The rice represented food and the loose change prosperity; I think the symbolism was that she'd have enough money and food in the New Year to be able to throw some away. I have no idea of the meaning of the herring.

The funny thing is, I never went downstairs the next day to see if the money was still there. I wondered, but I never went.

After she died, my family continued the tradition for a few years but finally stopped. I still eat herring on New Year's Eve, though I don't throw the rice and money out the window.

Al Parinello

Old Tappan, New Jersey

Private Little Blarney Stone

══╬╪══

Our family is large, Irish, and numbers quite a few writers among its members. There's not a famous name in the bunch, nor a rich one either, but two cousins work on local newspapers in their respective cities, an uncle and another cousin do industrial writing, my mother's been writing poetry all her life, and my brother and one sister are both freelance writers. Let's not even talk about my two frustrated playwright-uncles! And the cousin who has his own local band writes a lot of his own songs.

There is this stone that's been in the family for years, and the family story about it is that it's a chip off the Blarney Stone, brought over by a distant ancestor very late in the 1700s. Now, I don't believe for a minute that that stone was ever any part of the Blarney Stone, but my father says, "Who knows—anything is possible in this world. It could be," and my grandfather says, "Absolutely it's true! The story's been handed down through the family's generations, and it's true." So, who knows what's the truth of the matter?

There's a tradition around this stone, in any case. Allegedly the family's writing ability stems from the fact that every baby that's been born into the family has "kissed" our family's personal Blarney Stone. What actually happens is that the mother of a new baby in the family holds the freshly-washed stone to the infant's lips momentarily. No one in the family has dared deviate from the custom as yet, including a few very skeptical women who've married into the family.

Naturally, like most large families these days, we're not all living in the same city, or even the same state. So the stone's done a lot of traveling by US mail, UPS, and even FedEx. It's criss-crossed the country countless times, and was even shipped to Hawaii when a cousin who was living there for a year had a baby while there.

My wife is due to have our first child soon, and I won't be the one to break with tradition either. I don't for a minute believe either that that stone is a piece of the Blarney Stone or that it has anything to do with the writing ability that runs in the family, but when our child is born, I'm going to make sure my wife touches the stone to his or her lips if only for the sake of carrying on a charming family tradition.

Anonymous

A New Year's Dollar

Our family's New Year's Eve tradition is to put a dollar bill out-doors somewhere, making sure it's outside by the stroke of mid-night, so it's out there for the New Year. Any time after the clock strikes midnight, we can bring it in, and after that we leave it somewhere where we'll see it every day of the year that follows.

Every person in the household has to put out his or her own dollar bill, not just one for the whole family. On the following New Year's Eve, we each have to spend that dollar and put out a new one.

My parents have been doing this every year for at least forty-five years that I know of; they did it when I was a baby, and I believe that my grandparents did it too. The belief is that this will bring you good luck through the New Year, and is also so that you'll never spend your last dollar.

My father said that this is an old Scottish custom that my grandmother observed, which is strange since my grandmother is Ukrainian!

Pat Rogers
Alexandria, Virginia

"Fill Her Up, Moon"

Our family has a tradition we follow every month, at the time of the full moon. Every member of the family does this. You take your wallet out, open it up, look at the wallet, and say, "Fill her up, moon," three times. That's so that the moon will bring you good luck and fill up your wallet.

My mother still calls every month when she knows the full moon is coming and asks if we "filled her up."

Pat Rogers
Alexandria, Virginia

Mom's Superstitions

My mother believed in several of the more common superstitions—throwing salt over your shoulder if you spilled salt, to ward off bad luck, and never opening an umbrella in the house, as that would bring bad luck. But she also had three others that aren't as usual.

If anyone dropped silverware, she would say it meant company was coming, and the particular utensil dropped indicated specifically who the company would be: Dropping a spoon meant the visitor would be a child or someone young; a fork meant a woman; and a knife meant a man. She would be quite certain that the next person to ring the doorbell would be as predicted by the dropped silverware.

She also believed that women shouldn't whistle—more bad luck—and as her authority, she would quote the following poem:

> Whistling women
> And crowing hens
> Will bring a man
> To no good ends.

Last of all, she believed you should never put a hat on a bed. She realized the original rationale behind that was to avoid spreading head lice, but she was convinced it would bring bad luck.

She promoted her superstitions through the family all her life.

Jomil Mulvey
San Diego, California

Miscellaneous Customs and Traditions

So many of the "everyday" traditions are unclassifiable, but that doesn't make them any less valuable or enjoyable. They're not about holidays, not about birthdays, and in many cases not easily classifiable as "family harmony" or any other ready-to-apply label. Yet they're just as valuable, just as valid, just as important.

Here are some traditions and customs that were contributed to the book but that didn't fit into any of the other classifications yet certainly couldn't be omitted. Just as they found a "home" in this miscellaneous section, some of them may find a home with your family. Enjoy them.

Apples and Caring

⇒⊰⊱⇐

The house in which I grew up had a huge apple tree in the yard. My mother, an excellent baker, used to bake a huge quantity of apple pies using the apples off our own tree.

Of course our family was the beneficiary of a lot of her baking, but much of her output was given to shut-ins, mostly older people, to whom my mother herself delivered the pies, always finding time to stay for a little chat. Frequently she brought one or more of us children with her, explaining to us that the visit was about something more than just pies.

There were times, quite honestly, when we didn't want to accompany her, but Mom impressed on us the importance of caring about your fellow human being. "Mrs. So-and-so has nobody to talk to all day, and she doesn't get out anywhere. It would be a kindness to bring her a pie and some company," she'd say. So off we'd go with pies and conversation for an elderly or otherwise-shut-in person, and eventually we kids understood the importance of these visits.

I didn't inherit my mother's talent for baking well, but the house where I live now has a flower garden that I carefully tend, and I share my floral treats with shut-ins in our community. I've taught my kids the importance of these visits, too. Sometimes I get complaints from a child who'd rather hang out with friends or stay home and listen to music. Unlike my mother I don't insist on them accompanying me on these visits, but I've gotten the message across to them well enough that I'd say about fifty percent of the time at least one of my kids will go along with me.

I know our visits are valuable to the men and women we bring the flowers to—and not principally because of the flowers (as my mother taught me years ago). These visits are equally valuable for the character I'm trying to build in my children. Apparently I'm succeeding.

Anonymous

"Time Capsule" for Baby

When our granddaughter was born, my wife and I did something we think is rather unusual, which we hope will be meaningful to our grandchild as she grows older. We collected a "time capsule" for her.

In it—it's actually a large box—we put a newspaper from the day she was born, a couple of cassette tapes of popular music then at the "top of the charts" (not my wife's and my kind of music at all!), a women's magazine (with plenty of ads for currently trendy clothing), a few ads we'd recently received in the mail (to show prices for goods and services as of the time Caitlin was born), a couple of books from the best-seller list, and some items we came up with on our own:

We each (myself, my wife, my son, my daughter-in-law, and Caitlin's grandparents on the other side of the family) wrote out a "wish list" for Caitlin—exactly what we wished for her in her life, as she grew through childhood and into maturity. We also each wrote out a brief history of our own lives, so she would always have a record of her immediate ancestors, who they were, where they came from, what kind of people they were, and what their own childhoods were like. We also included a family tree from both sides of the family, showing as many branches and as far back as we could trace it.

There was also an extra piece of the wallpaper that covers the walls in Caitlin's room, a picture of the room and another of the outside of the house that she and her parents live in, pictures of all of us, taken three days after she was born, and a tape recording we all made about two weeks after she was born, each of us saying something to her that we hope will be meaningful to her as she grows up.

Now our daughter is pregnant, and we are already planning the contents of a time capsule for her baby when he's born.

Anonymous

Old Nickels

I grew up in a rather usual family; there were no big blasts out of the ordinary, except for our special treasures: "old nickels."

For some reason, my father believed that finding coins that were old, particularly nickels, was a very wondrous thing to do. After a week or so of saving the change we both wound up with, we would examine the coins. If one was "old," we would ceremoniously set it aside in a special jar designated just for old nickels.

These weren't coins that were valued as anything extraordinary; they were just ordinary, well-circulated old coins. But to my father and me, they were a rare find. As a child, I thought we were rich beyond measure because we were so wise to do this.

Although my father has passed away, and we no longer have an old nickel jar, I sometimes still find myself looking for the dates of coins in my change purse, putting the old ones aside. About a year or so ago, I went to put flowers on my father's grave and suddenly remembered the handful of old nickels I had been setting aside. I took them with me, dug into the earth near my father's headstone, dropped the nickels into the little hole I had made, and covered them up. Somehow those old nickels made me feel a little closer to my father.

Sure enough, my father had been right—I was rich, for I had the treasure of tradition.

Teresa Alexander
Hazel Park, Michigan

Barefoot Summer

Mayday—May 1—was always the first day of the year that kids were allowed to go barefoot. I have many happy memories of the first of May, when I could take off my shoes and socks, and run around barefoot everywhere (except to church or into town).

Of course we had to watch out for sharp items such as broken glass, and we had to be extra-careful in the barnyard, but these things became second nature to us.

This pleasant interlude lasted until the start of school on the day after Labor Day.

Herbert D. Tabor
South Houston, Texas

Family Customs and Traditions

The Hand Strikes Again!

Somewhere along the line, when I was a teenager, somebody in our family got a hold of a rubber hand and hid it around the house as a joke. That first time got good enough results that that hand got hidden again . . . and kept on getting hidden.

What had started as an ordinary practical joke actually evolved into a tradition within the family—specifically, that whoever found "the severed hand" said nothing to anyone but just hid it somewhere else for some other victim to discover. Silently each victim discovered it and was startled by it, and furtively he or she hid it for the next victim to discover.

That hand made its way into the freezer, turned up in various people's beds . . . there was no knowing where it would pop out next.

The tradition would probably still be going on but for the fact that my parents' marriage turned into a "commuter marriage," with my mom living with me, to help out, and my dad living in Arizona with my sister, and the two of them flying back and forth to see each other. The hand wound up in Arizona, so it hasn't jumped out at anyone lately.

Shannon Joplin
Seattle, Washington

"A Special Night"

What our children most enjoy, it seems, is what we call "A Special Night." We declare A Special Night for one family member or another on an average of about twice a month. My husband and I and the kids all get Special Nights.

Sometimes we declare A Special Night for one of the kids because of some accomplishment, such as if one son got an especially good report for behavior in Sunday School, or if the little one just learned to count all the way to fifteen. But sometimes we declare A Special Night for no particular reason at all; we want the kids to know we love and appreciate them even if they don't produce.

Special Nights are for us parents as well as the kids. A couple of nights ago, they seemed to think I was feeling discouraged, and they declared A Special Night for Mom. They got out the special plate and cup we always use. It's fine china with a dark blue trim and a Bible verse on it.

Before we say our prayer before dinner, we go around the table, with each person saying something about the person whose Special Night it is, something we appreciate about that person. The person whose night it is gets to choose the menu, too.

Sherry Yeaton
Epsom, New Hampshire

A Plate of Honor

I remember a special plate my mom made, which was for special occasions. It said something on it to the effect of: "You are special today" around the edges and was beautifully decorated. It was an honor to get to eat dinner off it.

The plate was used on birthdays, to honor someone for getting good grades or getting the lead in the school play, for sports accomplishments or winning science projects—things that are major accomplishments to children.

If we received especially good grades on tests and report cards, we always got a little treat of some kind.

Anonymous

Vacation Memorybooks

We take a family vacation every summer, and most years we take a few weekend trips as well. For the sake of posterity, we save souvenirs—and I don't mean hotel towels!—especially the kinds that can be saved between the pages of a scrapbook. (Not that I discourage the kids from saving shells during a trip to the shore, or anything else that won't fit into a scrapbook.) We make up a "memorybook" for every vacation, filling it with pictures and "flat souvenirs."

To augment the pictures we take, we also buy postcards and

include those in the scrapbook. (They came in especially handy the year something went wrong with the camera and none of the pictures came out. I always felt the flaw was with the photographer—my husband—not the camera itself, but that's another story.)

We've saved sugar wrappers with restaurant names on them, stubs from tickets to a theater where we saw a show in a town we were visiting, leaves and pressed flowers, brochures from tourist attractions . . . in short, virtually anything that would fit between the pages of a memorybook and remind us, in times to come, of some aspect of the trip we were on at the time.

It's fun to look back at the memorybooks and reminisce over trips past. The books have been our salvation more than once when a bored child was whining, "I've got nothing to do. I'm bored."

Anonymous

Artwork Hoax

There's a tradition in the family of a friend of mine that started as a joke and is still going on. When the family bought a pre-Civil-War home, they found among the junk in the basement an old statue, horribly ugly, that been created by an amateur—nobody famous. At first the decision was, "We're going to toss this," but then the mother fabricated a story around the statue.

She told the rest of the family that it was an old family heirloom that had been in the family for several generations and claimed it was one hundred years old. She even had a brass plate made up to affix to the statue, with a date on it that she picked arbitrarily.

Furthering the hoax, she started a tradition of passing the statue to a different member of the family every year, the ritual requiring that the family receiving it for the year display it. For forty years, this statue has passed annually from one family member to another. Everyone thinks it's ugly, but they all display it as required by this now-established tradition.

On her deathbed, the mother, who concocted the scheme, confessed all to her daughter, the only one in the family currently aware of the deception. She plans to pass the information on to her daughter in later years. Meanwhile, she's confided it in me.

The members of this family are scattered from the North Central part of the United States down to Florida, and every year some family member or another receives a crate with this ugly forty-year statue in it and is forced to display this "artwork" prominently for a year, never knowing that the whole tradition started with a hoax.

Phil Morris
Greensboro, North Carolina

Community Service

It started when our son did something he shouldn't have—I don't remember now what the infraction was, and really it's not important. The point is that, instead of our sending him to his room, suspending privileges, or something like that, we decided to give him a "community service" punishment, as the government does to some sentenced prisoners. So we told him he'd have to clean up the litter for one square block in our community.

Grudgingly he did it, but after the fact my wife and I got together and decided we'd made a wrong move. We'd assigned him community service as a punishment, and really community service should be something you do voluntarily out of wanting to make your community a better place to live.

My wife does charitable work; I give donations. It's never too early to educate kids about giving back to the world, about doing for other people.

So we decided that every Saturday we would each—my son, my wife, and myself—donate an hour to cleaning up as much litter as we could find in that time.

To make the task more pleasant, we told our son he could keep the money he could get from turning in all the cans he found, at a local recycling depot that pays for aluminum. We give him the cans we pick up, as well.

A few years ago, when we started this, we all went out as a family and did our community clean-up together. Now that our son is older, and can go around the neighborhood collecting trash alone, we don't go out as a unit; we're each free to do our share any hour that is convenient for us. As long as we each give an hour every Saturday.

Family Customs and Traditions

For a time, a few of the other kids laughed at our son, but because he makes money from the recycled cans, and because two other local families have taken a leaf from us and are now doing the same thing, the laughing has pretty much subsided.

Coming of Age in the Kitchen

My mom believed that at age fourteen, a child was no longer a child; part of this rite of passage involved responsibilities in the kitchen. Upon reaching the age of fourteen, all four of us— boys included!—were indoctrinated into the mysteries of the spice rack, the cookbook, and all that went with it.

Mom showed us her recipes, teaching us to cook the simpler stuff first, then working us up to more complex recipes. Prior to age fourteen, none of us had much to do with the stove or oven, beyond the very basic stuff, but at fourteen we were considered to be mature enough to learn to cook, and to do it right.

Because it was obviously a rite of passage, a coming-of-age marker, even my brothers didn't object too strenuously to being asked to learn to cook (though my younger brother begged the rest of us not to tell his friends—and when, inevitably, his brother told anyhow, he came in for a lot of kidding).

As each of us turned fourteen and learned to cook, he or she acquired the responsibility of cooking at least one dish a week for dinner, and preferably a whole meal once a week. (My mom would make allowances for heavy homework nights and such.)

Because my mom is a good cook, each of us learned to cook at least reasonably well. The real allure of the indoctrination, however, was that it made us each feel, when his or her turn came to learn to cook, that now we were truly grown up. (Knowing how to cook stood us all in good stead once we'd moved out and were living on our own. This didn't hit us till later, but it was much appreciated when we realized it.)

Anonymous

Pampering the New Mom

When any of my relatives (or friends) has a baby, I give the woman certificates for baby-sitting services, which I perform myself at a later date, or for massage from a massage therapist, or for some kind of pampering such as a facial. The baby-sitting certificates say that I will babysit a certain number of hours for her. When a baby is born, people often neglect the mother and concentrate on the baby. The mother needs attention and pampering too.

I also sometimes "kidnap" my nieces and my friends' kids, so the couple can go out and have a night on their own, and renew their romance.

Vicki L. Skinner
San Francisco, California

Parting Words

I had a Great-Uncle Horace who was a real gentle soul of an old man, but a bit of a blusterer too. When visitors would leave his house, he'd say to his wife, or whoever else was left in the house with them, "Damn glad they're gone!" He'd say it about the people he loved the most—I suppose it made the separation easier for him.

The custom carried down to my family. For instance, after family members who've come home to my parents' house for Christmas drive off again, those of us who are still left will say, "Damn glad they're gone!"

It's a family thing, said in a very loving way, but it shocked my husband the first time he heard it. He said, "Gayle, why did you guys say that? I thought they were very nice people!"

When Great-Uncle Horace finally died, the family was gathered at the cemetery, paying their last respects. One family member turned to the others and said, "Damn glad he's gone!"

Gayle Keane
Citrus Heights, California

Cousins' Club

≈⟨+⟩≈

If you saw the movie *Avalon*, you know all about cousins' clubs. They hold the family together. Our family had a cousins' club, formally known as the cousins' family circle. Well, actually we had two—one on my mother's side of the family and one on my father's. The person who had the largest house would host the club. The members would get together once every month or two.

Originally, way back, cousins' clubs were established to help relatives come to America and get settled. So there was already a tradition of cousins' clubs helping other members of the club and of the family.

Then, as families got Americanized, got busy, moved away from the city, and scattered, we still had an emotional tie among us cousins. Whole families came over from Europe to settle in America; their social life revolved around the extended family. Out of that grew these cousins' clubs.

They'd gossip, help relatives in distress, and plan the annual family cousins' club picnic. Everyone brought food to the picnic to share, and grills to cook on. We lived in Philadelphia, and we held our picnic in a park right outside the city. We had softball games and other games, all planned around the cousins.

Every few years, during one of our get-togethers, everyone would bring the oldest photographs they had, and we'd try to trace the family as far back as we could. We'd try to make connections with people and to figure out how we were all related to one another. New members were always joining the club, cousins who had grown old enough to participate. In later years, we grew to be such a large group that we gathered once a year at a country club and had a really fancy meal. We were gathering less and less often, and finally we stopped. It's a shame it died out.

It would be nice to renew the cousins' club contact again, so relatives could share the diversity we now have. But the relatives are scattered all over the country now.

Linda Becker
West Palm Beach, Florida

Family Names, Greek-Style

Our family names their children according to the old Greek tradition.

When the Greeks have children, the first-born male takes his first name from the father's father's name, and his middle name is the immediate father's first name. The second-born male child is named after the mother's father, also carrying the immediate father's first name as his middle name. The successive male children are named after the father's brothers or the mother's brothers, but also carrying the immediate father's first name as a middle name.

The girls are named the same way: The first-born girl is named after the father's mother, with her middle name being the father's first name. In our family, all seven kids are middle-named "John," even the girls!

Anonymous

Granny's Visitors

My granny had a tradition about visitors. She would always cook a good meal for you, whenever you visited her house, and then she wouldn't let you leave without taking something with you. It could be canned goods or something she'd cooked or baked, but she always would give you something before you left. She wouldn't let you leave her house without taking something with you.

Gracie Newsom
Benton, Tennessee

Theme Nights

One thing we've done in our family is theme nights. As an example, one evening we had a Hawaiian luau, complete with roast pork for dinner. We all dressed in appropriate clothing, such as muumuus. Our little boy wore swim trunks—this was mid-winter—and a touristy shirt to go with them. Our son has a collection of sea shells, so we scattered them across the table, along with some postcards from Maui that we have. We're not drinkers, but I made non-alcoholic daiquiris.

Other theme nights have been less elaborate but followed the same principle of the food, decorations, and so on, adhering to the theme of the evening.

Sherry Yeaton
Epsom, New Hampshire

San Sebastian Day

My wife of fifty-four years and I have a little something going that we call San Sebastian Day. It's not unique, but most people have never heard of it.

The origin of this tradition goes back to a high school class I was teaching. On a Friday afternoon prior to a home football game, the students would be excited and in no mood for studying. One time, one of the students said, "Mr. Halley, this is San Sebastian Day. Let's do something besides Geometry." So we celebrated San Sebastian Day in class.

Now whenever my wife and I are tired of the daily routine and want a break from it, we declare that it is San Sebastian Day, and we should celebrate it by suspending the routine and doing something we'd rather do instead, such as going out for dinner, or picking up a bottle of wine and visiting some friends.

Or if we want to give a person a gift when there is really no logical reason for it—we just want to—we present the gift as a San Sebastian Day gift.

Robert Halley
Laguna Hills, California

Family Customs and Traditions

Author's Note

Does your family have a tradition that's uniquely yours? If it does, and if you don't find something similar to it in these pages, why not send it along to me? If I get enough contributions, and if the response to this book is good enough, I'll follow up with *More Family Customs and Traditions*. Send your contributions of family traditions and customs to me at:

Cynthia MacGregor
5891 S. Military Trail - Suite 5-A
Lake Worth FL 33463

or E-Mail me at either
73043.1031@CIS.com
or CynMacG@AOL.com